SORRY
I RUINED
YOUR
ORGY

Praise for Bradley Sands

"Nothing I could dream up compares to the strangeness and wildness of Sorry I Ruined Your Orgy. You should read this book."
—Shane Jones, author of *Light Boxes*

"Sorry I Ruined Your Orgy is like an Adult Swim show written by Russell Edson."
—Carlton Mellick III, author of *The Faggiest Vampire*

"There's a place past all reason, most possibility, and all the jokes I can think of. A place shaped kind of like the human heart. Bradley Sands doesn't write about this place, but he writes from it, pushing farther into the unguessable with each word, each scene."
—Stephen Graham Jones, author of *Demon Theory*

"There is a disorienting alchemy at work in Sands' fiction."
—Rayo Casablanca, author of *6 Sick Hipsters*

"Sands is a talented, fearsome, comic visionary who will usher you into the psychedelic matrix of futurity."
—D. Harlan Wilson, author of *Dr. Identity*

"Reading the work of Bradley Sands caused me to vomit happiness from my eyeballs. Highly recommended."
—Kevin L. Donihe, author of *House of Houses*

Sorry I Ruined Your
Orgy

Bradley Sands

Lazy Fascist Press
Portland, OR

LAZY FASCIST PRESS
830 SW 18TH AVENUE
PORTLAND, OR 97205

WWW.LAZYFASCIST.COM

ISBN: 1-936383-15-2

ACKNOWLEDGMENTS

"Seth Schultz," "Brave Contestant of Faith," "Cormac McCarthy," and "Tao Lin" first appeared in *Spine Road*

"Eggs Benedict" first appeared in *NOÖ Journal* in a slightly different form

"Refrain" first appeared in *Zero Ducats*

"The Attic," "The Den," "The Study," and "The Laundry Room" first appeared in *Word Riot*

"Today Brandi Wells' Cat Fell Out of a Tree But He Was Not Upset" first appeared in *Brandi Wells Review*

"The Fall of Atlantis," "Bread and Body of Christ," "Debunking the Bard," and "How to Get Beautiful Women Into Bed" first appeared in *Olympus Found*

"A Suicidal Amputee Tries to Kill Himself by Rolling Off His Bed, Down the Stairs, Through the Screen Door, and Into Traffic; Some Dominican Kids Poke Him With Sticks Too, and an Eagle Shits on Him" first appeared in *Zygote in My Coffee*

"Want to Hear Something Really Creepy?" first appeared in *Twaddle Magazine*

"Magic Show" first appeared in *New Dead Families*

"A Sloth and the Newspaper Boy" first appeared *Wamack: A Journal of the Arts*

"Liquid Gold" first appeared in *Opium Magazine* in a slightly different form

"The Detective" first appeared in *No Colony*

"In the Airport" first appeared in *THE2NDHAND*

"The Adventures of a Small, Ceramic Giraffe in Tudor England" first appeared in *Kek-w Quarterly*

"Four Answers to Four Questions" first appeared in *(r)evolve: Naropa University Summer Writing Program Magazine*

"The Lunch Date" is forthcoming in *The Magazine of Bizarro Fiction*

"The Architects of the Dismantling" first appeared in *Mud Luscious* in a slightly different form.

"Archeologist" first appeared in *Lamination Colony*

"A Headless Man Falls in Love with a Bowl of Rice" first appeared in *Magazine of the Dead*

"In the Restaurant" first appeared in decomP, reprinted in *The &Now Awards: The Best Innovative Writing*

"Defeat of the Mountain Spirit" first appeared in *Micro 100*

"The Writer" appeared in *The Dream People*

CONTENTS

11   Seth Schultz

12   Eggs Benedict

14   Refrain

16   Brave Contestant of Faith

18   Temporomandibular

19   A Man Buys a Gun After Losing His Remote Control

20   The Attic

21   Today Brandi Wells' Cat Fell Out of a Tree But He
         Was Not Upset

23   The Fall of Atlantis

24   A Suicidal Amputee Tries to Kill Himself By Rolling
         Off His Bed, Down the Stairs, Through the
         Screen Door, and Into Traffic; Some Dominican
         Kids Poke Him With Sticks Too, and an Eagle
         and an Eagle Shits on Him

27   Want To Hear Something Really Creepy?

28   Magic Show

35   Going At It Like. . .

37   Electric Boogaloo

38   The Time Traveling Giraffe Is On Fire

39   Cormac McCarthy

41   Bread and Body of Christ

43   A Sloth and the Newspaper Boy

45   Liquid Gold

46   The Den

47   Tao Lin

49   The Detective

51   Birthday Present

52   Reading Sam Pink

53   Debunking the Bard

55   Hide and Seek Champion

56   In the Airport

59   The Adventures of a Small, Ceramic Giraffe in Tudor
      England

60   Four Answers to Four Questions

62   The Lunch Date

65   Time to Eat

66   The Ghost Parade

67   The Study

68   A Texas Cowboy and His Pal, The Genie, on Vacation

70   The Architects of the Dismantling

71   Archeologist

75   Caterpillars and Watermelons

76   A Headless Man Falls in Love with a Bowl of Rice

77   The Time Traveling Giraffe Defies God

78   In the Restaurant

80   Gathered in Nerdy Congress

81   The Laundry Room

82   Crawling Over Fifty Good Pussies to Get One Fat
           Boy's Asshole

90   Invincible

92   Alligator in Space

93   Scenes from the Life of a Greeting Card Designer

101   Defeat of the Mountain Spirit

102   One of Those Poorly Written Stories That Are
          Impossible to Follow Because There Are Too
          Many Goddamn Characters

104   Hold-up

106   The Writer

109   How to Get Beautiful Women Into Bed

110   Electronic Gaming News

SETH SCHULTZ

Seth Schultz goes to an orgy. He is not dressed appropriately. The invitation told him to come wearing nothing. He is wearing something. The man at the door tells him he cannot enter the orgy in a bear costume. Seth Schultz tears out the man's throat with his fake bear teeth and runs through the door growling. People stop who they are fucking to give Seth Schultz an opportunity to devour their innards. The next morning, the ghost of Seth Schultz's friend calls him on the telephone. She says, "I am among the things which shall not be spoken." Seth Schultz responds, "Sorry I ruined your orgy."

EGGS BENEDICT

for Mike Young

I am sitting by myself in a booth, eating Eggs Benedict. It is during peak hours. I have been eating the same breakfast for the past 72 weeks. The waitresses have started to give me dirty looks. Hungry, tableless people also give me dirty looks. A Tyrannosaurus rex sits down across from me. She is a very rude Tyrannosaurus rex. I say, "You are a very rude Tyrannosaurus rex. You should have asked if it was okay to sit at my table." The Tyrannosaurus rex does not respond. I leer at her. She feeds coins into the jukebox. Her eyes become fluorescent lights. Her teeth become a stack of menus. Her mouth becomes the door to the women's bathroom. She becomes the diner. The diner is sitting across from me. I feel lightheaded. The diner is a very rude diner. I say, "You are a very rude diner. You should have asked if it was okay to sit at my table." The diner asks for my hand in marriage. This catches me off guard. Women never ask me this question. I always ask this question. I weigh my options. I determine my response. I open my mouth to release it. The Eggs Benedict slips a diaphragm between its muffin and poached egg. This turns me on. I do not know why. Diaphragms do not usually have this effect on me. I have second thoughts about my response. I do not want to live in a world where I cannot take pleasure in a willing participant who is not my diner. The diaphragm turns into a puddle of Hollandaise sauce. A waitress touches my arm. She says, "I'm sorry, but we need your table." I look to the diner for guidance, but her seat is empty.

REFRAIN

The man walked on a city street. Above, a construction worker stood on a scaffold, thinking about his problems. He accidentally walked off the scaffold, fell. The worker landed, unharmed. The man's death bore the brunt of his weight. The death went like this: crunch, brightness, pressure, red vision, fade.

No, it did not happen this way.

The man walked on a country road. He wore an eye patch over his left eye. It was the only thing preventing him from seeing. A car drove nearby with the radio on. A song played. It was not good. The driver agreed. She turned the knob. She turned the wheel. The car's bumper forced the man on the ground. Its front right tire crushed his throat. The death went like this: sensation, smother blind, no breath.

We have it wrong again.

The man walked on the moon. He wore an eye patch over his eye. It was the only thing preventing him from seeing. He liked pirates. He sacrificed his peripheral vision to his interests. Another man was on the moon. He was not in it. The other man wondered how the man ended up on the moon, how he was able to breath. He was not able to breath. He clutched his chest, stopped walking. Stopped breathing. The death went like this: frazzle, no breath.

This is only what they want you to think.

The man walked down his driveway, got into his car. He wore an eye patch over his eye. It was the only thing preventing him from seeing. He liked pirates. He sacrificed his peripheral vision to his interests. He put the car in reverse, thought about the treasure hidden in his walls. When he reached the end of the driveway, he turned the wheel, backed out some more, put the car in drive, turned right. He drove, started to make his first left, crossed over the opposite lane, thought about parrots with big mouths. A car smashed into his right side, pushed him into the front of a stopped bus. The death went like this: plastic bubbles, red vision, "Is my head coming off?"

"Yes, it is."

Fuck all this lying.

The man walked up a mountain. He wore an eye patch over his eye. It was the only thing preventing him from seeing. He liked pirates. He sacrificed his peripheral vision to his interests. His bathtub at home was filled with grog. So was his canteen. He took a sip, gagged. He reached the top of the mountain, sat, stared, felt awed by the beauty of the horizon. Stood up, walked down, got into his car, drove home. The life went like this: joy, bills, sorrow, weariness, contentment, quest for the perfect last words.

BRAVE CONTESTANT OF FAITH

for xTx

Jack is a contestant on the game show, God or No God. He is starving and would like to win a million dollars to end his hunger. Jack's chair hangs above a 20-car pileup. While his astral body sits in the chair, his physical body is embedded in a car windshield. Jack's hand is on a buzzer. He is waiting for Chuck Barrett to ask a question. Chuck Barrett does not exist. If Jack does not answer Chuck Barrett's non-existent question correctly, he will be ejected from his chair. He will be hurled into a different state. A state between shards and nothingness. If he does answer Jack Barrett's non-existent question correctly, he will be able to buy many loaves of bread. Chuck Barrett asks his non-existent question. The non-existent question has a non-existent answer. Jack does not know the answer because it is non-existent. Since his hunger would prefer many loaves of bread over a state between shards and nothingness, he prays to God. He asks God to reveal the non-existent answer. He promises he will share his loaves of bread with God in return for His wisdom. He waits for God's answer. But God does not speak. Instead, God comes down from the heavens and tap dances and causes earthquakes and envy. Then God's head turns into a balloon, separates from His body, and rises. God's torso falls down in the dirt. Jack's time runs out. God's tap dancing routine and ascension have not helped him answer Chuck Barrett's non-existent question. He swallows the shards and they taste like earwax-flavored Starburst and he repents of his sins.

TEMPOROMANDIBULAR

There is a kitten in my mouth
I cannot go to sleep without her in my mouth
or I wake up with pain in my head

She is not really a kitten
She is something so dull that
I feel the urge to tell you she is a kitten

Sometimes when I'm relaxing
I start to nod off
and I need to wake myself up and put the kitten in my mouth
or face the consequences

My life was so much better before I had to go through the intricate ritual
of putting a kitten in my mouth at bedtime

It takes a long time to catch her

A MAN BUYS A GUN AFTER LOSING HIS REMOTE CONTROL

The man has been watching *Everybody Loves Raymond* reruns for the last ten years. He has been looking for his lost remote for the last ten years. His remote is not underneath the couch cushions. His remote is not in the refrigerator. His remote is not floating in the clouds. The man has given up on finding the remote, but not on the possibility of watching a show that isn't *Everybody Loves Raymond*. He goes to the gun shop. Buys a gun. Goes home. Sits on the couch. Loads the gun. Puts it next to his head. Changes the channel. The man finds it difficult to watch Seinfeld reruns with his brains all over the screen.

THE ATTIC

Dad is the only family member who has been in the attic. It is where he keeps his second family. He has warned his wife and sons not to go up there. "The floor is filled with holes. You need to know where to step or you will fall. I know where to step. I will never fall." Dad sometimes brings things up to the attic. They are things the family does not need but feels bad about throwing out. He relocates these items so his family will never suspect the attic is anything but a storage space. He relocates these items so his other family has objects that remind them of their existence. Some fathers escape to the movies after having loud arguments with their wives. Dad relocates items to the attic and spends the night with his conflict-free backup family.

TODAY BRANDI WELLS' CAT FELL OUT OF A TREE BUT HE WAS NOT UPSET

for Brandi Wells

The tree grows bitter fruit. It does not enjoy its flavor. It washes away the taste by snickering at the atrocities of gravity. Children like to climb its branches. They do not like to fall down, but they cannot help it. They cannot help bleeding and crying. The tree nourishes itself on blood and tears. Blood and tears wash away the bitter fruit. Blood and tears are delicious and overwhelming.

Brandi Wells' cat does not like to bleed and cry. Brandi Wells' cat likes to climb trees. When he climbs a tree, he does not see a tree filled with bitter fruit. He sees friendly bee squishy toys hanging off its branches. Brandi Wells' cat makes nice with a friendly bee. He makes it go squishy. He makes it go squeak. He makes it go squishy and squeak and he loses his footing. He falls out of the tree. The tree prepares to wash away its bitterness. But Brandi Wells' cat does not bleed. Brandi Wells' cat does not cry. Brandi Wells' cat is not upset. He is not an atrocity of gravity. While the falling children felt air and emptiness, Brandi Wells' cat made nice with a parachute of sunshine in an atmosphere of cotton candy.

THE FALL OF ATLANTIS

It is beautiful outside. The beauty makes Atlantis want to go outside for a walk. Atlantis is already outside. It just needs to start walking. It needs to tear itself from the ground. So Atlantis tears itself from the ground. Atlantis's denizens are not happy about Atlantis tearing itself from the ground. But Atlantis's denizens will have to learn to deal with Atlantis tearing itself from the ground. It is beautiful outside. Atlantis walks through jungles of caterpillar and deserts of ostrich and forests of elephant and alleys of pterodactyl. Upon reaching a field of bricks, Atlantis is pushed by Push the bully. Atlantis falls. Its denizens die. But Atlantis's denizens will have to learn to deal with dying. It is beautiful outside.

A SUICIDAL AMPUTEE TRIES TO KILL HIMSELF BY ROLLING OFF HIS BED, DOWN THE STAIRS, THROUGH THE SCREEN DOOR, AND INTO TRAFFIC; SOME DOMINICAN KIDS POKE HIM WITH STICKS TOO, AND AN EAGLE SHITS ON HIM

for Jereme Dean

The suicidal amputee's legs are playing a video game. The video game is called God Abuse. It is in two-player mode.

The suicidal amputee's left leg is trying to get the amputee to kill himself by rolling off his bed, down the stairs, through the screen door, and into traffic.

The suicidal amputee's right leg is trying to convince him that he has everything to live for.

The suicidal amputee's left leg is evil.

The suicidal amputee's right leg is good.

The suicidal amputee's left leg presses up on the control pad to roll him out of bed.

The suicidal amputee's right leg pushes the B button to make him think about the wetness of a hooker's mouth.

The suicidal amputee's left leg presses down on the control pad to roll him down the stairs.

The suicidal amputee's right leg pushes the Z button to make him think about the cheapness of Baron Rothschild Vodka.

The suicidal amputee's left leg presses right on the control pad to roll him through the screen door.

The suicidal amputee's right leg pushes the B button to make him think about the time he shot a gook in the face.

The suicidal amputee's left leg presses left and then down on the control pad to roll him into traffic.

The suicidal amputee's right leg presses up up down down on the control pad and the X button and the A button and the Y button and the B button to turn the suicidal amputee into a monster truck.

The suicidal amputee's left leg presses left on the control pad to make him crush cars and extinguish lives.

The suicidal amputee's right leg pushes the X and Y buttons at the same time until the drivers' screams fill his heart with joy.

The suicidal amputee's left leg pushes the start button and the pause button at the same time to make some Dominican kids poke him with sticks and an eagle shit on him.

The suicidal amputee's right leg taps rapidly on the B button until he doesn't care about the Dominican kids or the eagle shit because his heart has exploded all over the black asphalt.

WANT TO HEAR SOMETHING REALLY CREEPY?

I wrote this on a couch,
not my couch.
A couch of undeterminable origin
in an unknown terrain.
I wanted to write this on my couch
but after sitting down on my couch
and beginning to write
I was no longer on my couch
but on someone else's.

MAGIC SHOW

Detective watches the magic show. The amphitheater could hold ten thousand people, but he is the only person in the audience. He wonders if Magician would stop the show if he were to get up to leave. Curiosity overtakes him. He stands, waves to Magician and Lovely Assistant as he walks down the aisle. He leaves through the door. The usher with the red fedora has vanished. Perhaps Magician has made him disappear? Detective opens the door a crack, peeks inside. Magician has not stopped the show. But what happened to the rabbit in the hat trick? Magician was performing the trick when Detective exited the theatre. He had only just started the trick by extending his top hat towards Detective to prove it was an ordinary top hat.

Instead of the rabbit in the hat trick, Magician has made the ceiling vanish and the stars turn into flying giraffes and the flying giraffes attack the Earth. Detective is not impressed. He has seen other magicians perform this trick before. He has seen flying giraffes attack the Earth before. He has seen the Earth covered in blood that spouted out of people's necks after flying giraffes devoured their faces. Detective is not impressed.

He crashes through the door, shakes his fist, shouts, "I am not impressed!" His words echo through the amphitheater.

Magician ignores his complaints, holds out Rabbit for Detective to inspect.

But what happened to the flying giraffes attacking the Earth trick? Detective is confused. He uses the full extent of his analytical mind to determine what happened to the flying giraffes attacking the Earth trick, comes up empty.

Magician puts Rabbit in a top hat, taps the top hat with his wand, says Magic Words, makes the animal disappear. Lovely Assistant waves her arms excitedly. Whoa, Detective thinks, What happened to the rabbit? He uses his analytical mind to determine where the creature went, fails. He is ashamed of himself, wonders if he should stop calling himself a detective. If he is unable to solve a mystery, he should probably refer to himself by another title. His customers are not willing to pay him fifty bucks a day plus expenses for him to feel ashamed when he is unable to solve their problems. Perplex-tive, he thinks. He needs to get all new business cards so they read, John Johns—Perplex-tive for hire. People will pay him to be perplexed. There are so many people in the world. Some of them must want to take advantage of a service where he provides his bewilderment on demand.

Magician taps the black top hat with his wand, says Magic Words, pulls Rabbit out of the top hat. Lovely Assistant waves her arms excitedly. "Whoa," Detective says out loud this time while clutching his heart. The shock of Rabbit's return almost gives him a heart attack. But it does not give him a heart attack, because he has a healthy diet and exercises on a regular basis. Since he is not dead, Detective claps furiously to show his appreciation for Magician's ability to leave him perplexed. Detective pumps his fist in the air, hoots, stamps his foot on the floor. Magician and Lovely Assistant bow. They freeze and do not move. Detective waits, wondering if the show is over or if Magician and Lovely Assistant are trying to delight him with their showroom dummy impersonations. Detective is not delighted. He is a little bored. But he is also a little mystified.

He cannot understand how a person can stand so still. He is mystified that two people in the world can stand this still. He is even more amazed that these two still people are standing on the same stage. How did they find each other? Did one of them take out a classified ad?

Detective walks towards the stage, climbs the steps, taps on Magician's padded shoulder. "Errr . . . excuse me." Magician does not stir, so Detective tries the same thing on Lovely Assistant's shoulder. "Errr . . . excuse me." She is not receptive. Detective is frustrated. He is ashamed at his inability to cause motion. He goes back to Magician, licks his earlobe.

Magician flinches. "Who dares disturb Merrigan the Magnificent?"

"Me."

"Who is me? Who dares?"

"Name's Ray Smith. I'm a private dick. Got a few questions for you." He hands Magician his card.

"Proceed at your own risk, mortal."

"Where were you on the night someone finished my milk and did not replace it?"

"A magician cannot be compelled to reveal his whereabouts subsequent to his birth and prior to his death."

Detective opens his coat to give Magician a view of his gun. "Tell me or I will make your life vanish and never reappear."

"I do not respond to threats, Mr. Smith, particularly of the gunshot wound-kind considering I am bulletproof."

"Oh yeah?" He pulls his gun out of his holster, puts it to Magician's forehead, pulls the trigger.

Magician's brains rocket out of the back of his skull. They splatter over his Cabinet of Secrets.

Detective feels bad. It is the first time he has killed a man. He believed Magician was bulletproof. It is not his fault. Magician told him he was bulletproof. Detective has always wanted to shoot a man who was bulletproof. This was his first opportunity, although it was a false opportunity. Detective frowns, regretting he took the opportunity. He puts his gun back in its holster.

Lovely Assistant stirs. "What's going on here?"

"I killed him. I feel terrible about it."

Lovely Assistant stares at Magician's corpse, Magician's brains. "Don't worry, he's bulletproof."

Detective also stares at the brains. "If he's bulletproof then my name's Ray Brainsplatter."

"It's nice to meet you, Mr. Brainsplatter. Merrigan the Magnificent doesn't look bulletproof. Is that correct?"

Detective is getting exasperated. "Yes."

"Are you ready for Merrigan the Magnificent's brain matter to return to its former location? Are you ready for Merrigan the Magnificent to arise from his deep slumber?"

"Yeah, whatever."

She pries Magician's wand out of his dead hand, taps his skull, says Magic Words.

Magician's brains grow little feet and walk from The Cabinet of Secrets to the back of his skull and his skin and hair grow over the exit wound and his blood becomes invisible and he opens his eyes.

Lovely Assistant reaches out her arms, wiggles her fingers, says, "Ta-da!"

Detective feels a sense of fulfillment. He has shot a man who was bulletproof. He can cross out this item on the list of the countless things he wants to do before he dies.

Detective says, "That was pretty swell, but did you drink the rest of my milk?"

Magician curls his upper lip in disdain. "The milk of mortals causes disgust and digestive troubles. My liquid diet is entirely composed of ambrosia and pigeon blood. I would rather kiss my lovely assistant than ingest your vile cow juice."

"Yeah, my roommate is probably the culprit if you didn't do it. Let's get down to serious business: Where does the rabbit in your hat go after it disappears?"

"A magician never reveals his secrets."

Detective opens his coat to give Magician a view of his gun, remembers Magician is bulletproof, frowns, puts the gun back in the holster. "You gotta tell me. It's a matter of life and death."

"I, Merrigan the Magnificent, imbibe such an enormous quantity of life and death that my tolerance has achieved the height of the cosmos."

Detective puts Magician in a headlock. "I'm tired of your mystical mumbo jumbo. If you wanna get outta this headlock, tell me where the damn rabbit goes."

"I am not the man in the headlock but you are the man in the headlock."

Detective stares into Magician's eyes, but they are not Magician's eyes—they are Detective's Eyes, surrounded by Detective's face. He squeals and releases his phantom double from the headlock. The phantom double regains the features of Magician.

Lovely Assistant waves her arms excitedly. "Let's hear it for Merrigan the Magnificent."

Magician points at Detective with his long finger and engages in a round of sinister laughter. "I will grace your query with a response if you perform a service for me. Walk across the entirety of this stage and the secret of the rabbit shall be revealed."

Detective begins walking, is stopped by an invisible force. The force feels like a chainsaw. Detective's insides feel like they are being torn apart by a chainsaw, but his body does not have any wounds. It does not release blood. Perhaps Magician has made Detective's blood and wounds invisible?

Detective considers turning back, decides against it. The location of Rabbit is more important to him than answers to questions like "Is there life after death?" and "Is there other life in the universe?" and "Why me?" The answer is worth the loss of invisible blood and invisible viscera. He tries to crawl through the chainsaw pain, but it does not allow him to proceed. He tries over and over again but it is futile. Frustrated, he bangs his head on the floor. It makes a hollow sound. He knows the difference between a hollow sound and a filled sound. He notices a latch in the floor, bangs his head in frustration. A skilled detective would have noticed the latch, realized he was lying on top of a trapdoor, avoided further incidents with chainsaw pain. He thinks about the chainsaw pain. The thought of the pain knocks him unconscious.

When Detective wakes up, he is lying onstage in the same place where he lost consciousness. He had expected a boiler room and a chair and ropes tied around him, but that only happens to real detectives. Detectives like him wake up in the same place they lose consciousness. There is no pockmarked ex-boxer slapping his face and asking questions. There is only Magician and Lovely Assistant and the void. He opens the trapdoor.

Climbs down some steps.

Floats past a universe composed of Legos.

Swims through an ocean of thumbtacks.

Climbs a mountain of spleens.

Why is Detective doing all these things? Why are all these things under the stage? A trapdoor in a stage should lead to a small passageway to crawl through. A passageway of wood rather than Legos, thumbtacks, and spleens. It is difficult to travel through Legos and thumbtacks and spleens. It is difficult, but worth it. Detective would crawl through thousands, maybe millions, of miles of nuclear flame to discover the location of Rabbit. When Detective's head peeks out of a crater in the stage, he's glad he didn't have to crawl through nuclear flame. He would not have appreciated that.

Detective lifts himself out of the crater, and Magician says, "I congratulate you on your triumph, Mr. Smith."

Detective twitches his eyebrows. "Where is it?"

"Where is what?"

"Where is the rabbit?"

"Why would you like to know?"

"I've got no idea."

"I will tell you since you chanced the treacheries of the trapdoor."

"Do it."

"The rabbit never left the hat. You merely failed to observe him."

Detective pulls his gun out of his holster, puts it to Magician's forehead, pulls the trigger.

Lovely Assistant says, "Ta-da!"

GOING AT IT LIKE . . .

They were drilling for carrot juice, battering-ramming down the door to the fleshy fortress, churning love-butter, giving immunization shots to prevent the extinction of the species, doing the sort of thing a babysitter isn't paid enough to deal with when taking her charges to the park.

"Bunnies silly!" shouted Benjy, then he spun his four-year-old tongue around as if it were the propeller of a helicopter.

"What are the rabbits doin'?" asked his older sister, Wendy.

The babysitter sighed. "They're giving each other colon exams."

Wendy looked perplexed. "What's a colon exam?"

"That's when someone is made extremely uncomfortable for the purpose of detecting cancer at an early stage."

A furry couple were each sitting in a swing, grasping the opposite sides of the swing set. After snorting to three, they let go and the two swings bombarded into each other, giving the male rabbit's enormous . . . carrot . . . the opportunity to visit his mate's rabbit hole. Then the swings parted, the rabbits returned to their opposite sides by pushing at the ground with their feet, and the countdown began anew.

Benjy looked at the flying lovers and said, "I wanna play with the bunnies!"

"You'll have to wait your turn. But before that happens, I'll have to disinfect your swing."

Wendy stared, hypnotized, at a moving wall of fornication: bunnies straddling, grappling, snatch-assing, sucking, and bucking. "Why are they pushing each other?"

"They're angry that their mommies and daddies like their brothers and sisters better than them."

The little girl smiled and said, "Oh, I thought they were just fucking."

ELECTRIC BOOGALOO

The man is skinny and tall. He is spinning on his shaved head. His head is not bleeding because he is spinning on a piece of cardboard. The piece of cardboard was torn off a box that once housed a punching bag. The man is spinning like a dreidel and preparing for takeoff. He is communicating with ground control. They say, "Take off initiated. Begin countdown." Hip hop beats explode out of the man's ghetto blaster. An MC counts backwards from ten. Fire shoots out of the man's head, and it releases the sound of an explosion. The MC says, "Lift off" and the man blasts into space, grabbing stars as he passes and clutching them to his chest.

THE TIME TRAVELING GIRAFFE IS ON FIRE

Men and women dance to the black plague. The time traveling giraffe does not mind the flames. They make him feel special. He is the only burning giraffe in the universe. He is the only giraffe who exists simultaneously in every point in history. The time traveling giraffe has never actually time traveled. His gastric juices have time traveled. Time travelers he has ingested have time traveled. The time traveling giraffe only burns. He must always feed the fire. He is the loneliest giraffe on earth.

CORMAC MCCARTHY

The alleyway lacks light but it is day and the stars in the sky provide illumination for Cormac McCarthy to view the buildings' walls which are covered by posters depicting the image of a man who is unknown to him and a woman yells out the window in a voice of dissonance and Cormac McCarthy runs out of view towards the front of the building. But instead of the front of the building there is only an empty lot filled with transparent dirt that exhibits the bodies of those who argued with the existence of the dirt's transparency and since Cormac McCarthy is skeptical he walks beyond the territory where the transparent dirt has authority and the place looks like an empty white room without furniture but is actually the fertile land where farmers grow trombones and he tries to pick an instrument for his personal use because he is a talented jazz musician but he looks into his hand and sees empty white space and a lack of furniture and he is delighted because a trombone creates the bellow of an elephant which is a sound that his ears are allergic to and prolonged exposure will cause them to revert to their original state of being cauliflower and he leaves the empty white room and passes a man who is outside walking his house on a leash and Cormac McCarthy wonders if this walk will produce urine or feces or wood shavings and he nods to the man grimly knowing the fate of a man who believes in the plausibility of walking his own house and the house barks at him and he is afraid of this criticism of his presence so he turns onto Everything Street and is dismayed to discover everything blocking his path and he makes mean faces at everything but it does not budge and Cormac McCarthy calls his wife to tell her he will be late for supper.

BREAD AND BODY OF CHRIST

Richard F. Huffenstern is suing the Pope. He didn't sign up for Catholicism to drink cheap wine and eat round flat bread. He signed up for Catholicism so he could cannibalize the son of God and vampirize his rapid beard-growing superpowers. Richard F. Huffenstern is disappointed. Richard F. Huffenstern is a high-priced New York City lawyer. Richard F. Huffenstern is suing the Pope for false advertising.

The Pope is given a summons to appear in court. A DNA report is stapled to the document. Richard F. Huffenstern has hired laboratory technicians to determine the paternity of a piece of round flat bread and twelve fluid ounces of cheap wine. The laboratory results have determined that flour is the round flat bread's mother, water its father. It has also determined that the wine's mother is a grape, its father a strain of yeast.

Richard F. Huffenstern gets his day in court. The Pope is on the stand. He is wearing a funny hat. Richard F. Huffenstern is questioning him. Richard F. Huffenstern is asking hard-hitting questions. The Pope has a bloody nose. He looks flustered. Richard F. Huffenstern asks him to explain why he did not get the opportunity to drink the blood and eat the body of Christ when it was promised to him in the glossy brochure.

The Pope blurts out, "Because God doesn't exist, you nimrod!"

God comes down from the Heavens, hires Richard F. Huffenstern, and sues the Pope for false representation. Richard F. Huffenstern tells God his hourly rate is a little of his son's flesh and a little of his son's blood.

A SLOTH AND THE NEWSPAPER BOY

for Grant Wamack

A wager. Twenty bucks says a sloth can be a sloth faster than the newspaper boy can be the newspaper boy. You're on! The sloth sloths slowly. The newspaper boy delivers papers quickly. You scowl. You take out a cell phone and place a call. A pit bull with a cell phone chases the newspaper boy. Its saliva eats through the newspaper boy's bicycle. I call shenanigans. You put a gun in my mouth. I stop calling shenanigans. The sloth sloths slowly. The newspaper boy delivers newspapers on foot. The pit bull's saliva has not eaten through his positive outlook. You scowl. You take out a detonator and push a button. The paperboy's Nikes go bang. The explosion eats through his limbs. I call shenanigans. You open a manhole to reveal the sewers and a cage. A hungry alligator is in the cage. My family is in the cage. I stop calling shenanigans. The sloth sloths slowly. The newspaper boy crawls to his next delivery. The explosion has not eaten through his positive outlook. You walk into a secret control room and go through the motions of dropping an atom bomb on the newspaper boy's head. The atom bomb eats through his everything. I call shenanigans. You cover The Light with a blackout curtain. I stop calling shenanigans. The sloth sloths slowly. The newspaper boy has stopped being a newspaper boy. The atom bomb has eaten away at his positive outlook. I frown. I give you twenty bucks. You rush off to spend it on absolutely nothing.

LIQUID GOLD

Captain Thumbtack looks for buried treasure up his nose. He pokes through an ocean of decaffeinated coffee, prods a bipolar sea monster, bests the Rubber Duckie armada in combat, lands on a desserted island, stabs into the cakey earth, uncovers a gorilla chest, participates in an exciting battle with his crew over the identity of the chest's owner, discovers his men consist of a drugstore's hand mirror display, cleans his wounds with brake fluid, and unlocks the gorilla with his thumbtack's skeleton key-like attributes. A spurt of blood shoots out of the captain's nose. It lands in a funnel welded into an arm belonging to the pirate's son. The boy resuscitates. The blood flows into an open vein. He gets a little purple back into his face. The blood continues to spit across the room. The pirate waits. He watches a program on bass fishing. The host sits in a rowboat for 30 minutes. Sometimes the pirate can make out a wave. The credits roll. The blood transfusion is complete. Captain Thumbtack's son leaps into his arms. The pirate presents his son with a toothy grin. The boy is disgusted by his father's poor dental hygiene. His arm vomits out a swimming pool-worth of blood. The son dies, reaching for an electric toothbrush.

THE DEN

The man remembers the crack in the wall. When he was a boy, he looked through the crack and told his father what he saw. He said, "I saw a room I have never seen before. Neon triangles covered the wallpaper. There was a fuzzy pink rug on the floor. A table and chair were beside the rug. On the table was an empty glass." The father said, "You're not supposed to know about that room. It belonged to my father." The boy was confused because his father's father never lived in his house. The father did not react to the perplexed look on his son's face. Instead he got his toolbox out of the closet and fixed the crack. The next time the boy tried to look through the crack, he was a man.

TAO LIN

Tao Lin drinks an ape-flavored smoothie. The ape is displeased. He punishes Tao Lin by giving him the ability to turn his eyebrows into gold. Tao Lin turns his eyebrows into gold. He tries to shave them off so he can afford a gourmet tofu dog at an expensive downtown restaurant. The Bic razor is powerless against the precious metal. Tao Lin is frustrated. Tao Lin wants a chainsaw. He cannot find a chainsaw in Brooklyn, so he takes a train to Long Island. It stops in Long Island and Tao Lin breaks into someone's garage to chainsaw off his eyebrows. It is graphic. Inappropriate for a general audience. But his wounds are also inappropriate for expensive downtown restaurants, and when he goes to one of them to spend his gold eyebrows on a gourmet tofu dog, the attractive hostess refuses him entry. He goes to a hospital to make his wounds appropriate for an expensive downtown restaurant, but he does not have insurance. Full-time writers do not have insurance. So he offers his gold eyebrows in exchange for appropriateness. The nurse says, I'm sorry but we only accept cash check or credit card. Tao Lin goes to a bank to exchange his eyebrows for hundred dollar bills. He bleeds on the teller. The man punches him in the face. Tao Lin makes a neutral facial expression to avoid the embarrassment of tears. The teller to the left feels sorry for him. She feels sorry for him because she is very old and has suffered through many inappropriate wounds. She says, It is usually against bank policy to exchange gold for currency but I will make an exception because you look like my cute little hamster. Tao Lin accepts the money and spends all of it on appropriateness. He is sad that he can no longer afford a gourmet tofu dog. Feeling existentially fucked, Tao Lin goes home to wait for his eyebrows to grow back.

THE DETECTIVE

The detective is paid two hundred bucks a day plus expenses to locate a man's lost TV remote. He goes to an electronics store to find out more information. A salesman is wearing a suspicious cleft palate. The detective clears his throat and spits a fifty into the salesman's palm. The salesman puts a box into a bag, hands the bag to the detective. The detective looks inside the bag. The detective looks inside the box. A portable television is inside the box. The portable television is powered by hyperactive hamsters. The detective says, "My fifty dollars was for information, not portable televisions powered by hyperactive hamsters." The salesman looks suspicious. The detective punches him in the nose. The salesman tells the detective that his store is having a sale on 42 inch flat screen TVs. He tells them they are priced at his immortal soul for a limited time only. The detective castrates the salesman with a machete. He says, "My fifty dollars was for information pertaining to the whereabouts of my client's lost TV remote, not your weekly sales." The salesman sings, "Oooooh," in a beautiful voice. He gets to the chorus: "Has he checked inside his refrigerator?" The detective takes out his cell phone and calls his client. "Have you checked inside your refrigerator?"

The client checks inside his refrigerator. His remote control is next to a jar of peanut butter. The detective earns his two hundred bucks, plus fifty-five dollars for expenses.

BIRTHDAY PRESENT

for Ian Sands

I needed to get my brother a present for his birthday. I could not figure out what to get. I considered a giant lobster named Eduardo. The giant lobster named Eduardo was not very cooperative. He said, "I am not a birthday present. Why don't you get your brother the moon and the stars?" I tried to give my brother the moon and the stars for his birthday, but I could not fit them into a box. I decided to give him an empty box that was large enough to hold everything in existence except for the moon and the stars. I fell into the box. This made it even more difficult to figure out what to get my brother for his birthday. I was in an empty box, so I had very limited choices: emptiness or emptiness. So I chose a pair of socks with a family of happy piranha sewn onto the seams.

READING SAM PINK

The book decides to read Sam Pink. It opens his chest cavity and reads the first entrail. It is a very good first entrail. It makes the book very excited. It captures the book's attention and does not let go. The book's attention tries to escape, but it is caught in Sam Pink's razor wire chest hair. The book turns the artery. The phone rings. The book uses Sam Pink's penis to mark its place and sews him up. The book answers the phone. It is the book's mother, the wise old tree. The book masturbates while speaking to her because it thinks it is a funny thing to do. The book ejaculates and hangs up the phone. The book picks up Sam Pink again. It reads about a red blood cell's exciting adventures in a haunted ice box. Sam Pink yells in a scary way. Sam Pink has had enough. Sam Pink burns the book with his heat vision. Sam Pink puts the fire out by pissing on it. Sam Pink opens the book and shits on page 62.

DEBUNKING THE BARD

The academic in front of the hot dog stand says, "William Shakespeare did not write any of the plays attributed to William Shakespeare."

The hot dog vendor serves the academic a hot dog and says, "Fuckin' A, guy. Tell me something I don't know."

The academic bites into the hot dog, chews, swallows, and says, "Leatherface chainsaw-massacred William Shakespeare and wore his flesh as a mask while he wrote the world's greatest literature."

The hot dog vendor spits into the academic's face and says, "You're just trying to trick me. Leatherface wasn't around back when Shakespeare was writing all those namby-pamby 'oooh look at me, tee and thee is so fucking poetry' buttsex fests."

William Shakespeare erupts out of the hot dog stand, waving a chainsaw. Blood spurts over the hot dogs. The chainsaw transforms the hot dog vendor into a pile of organs. William Shakespeare says, "Gnaaaaarrrrl."

The academic looks star-struck. He says, "I'm a big fan of your work, Leatherface."

William Shakespeare tears off his face. He tears off the academic's face. He slips the William Shakespeare face over the academic's skull. He slips the academic's face over his own skull.

William Shakespeare and the academic hold hands and skip off to a wedding chapel.

HIDE AND SEEK CHAMPION

He hides in the ground. Liquid granite shoots through his veins, escapes through his pores. The gravestone sprouts out from the dirt. He does not. He lies there until his epitaph develops on the stone. He lies there some more.

IN
THE
AIRPORT

Nobody will tell us why our flight has been delayed. We are very disgruntled.

Is there someone else we can speak to? A supervisor?

Oh, you are the supervisor? We feel an urge to murder you, but choose to keep our emotions trapped beneath the skin since we are civilized people, unlike you and your employees. Anyone who treats their customers this way is a barbarian.

Why are you preventing us from holding our loved ones in our arms? We haven't seen them in months.

Yes, we understand all the planes have been delayed. You've made it clear. There's nothing you can do. No, we don't want a magazine and a beverage from the airport gift shop. We demand an explanation.

You're blaming the weather? That's ridiculous. It might be winter, but there's not a snowflake in the sky.

No, we haven't looked out the window lately. We will do that now, after we're done visualizing your head as it flies through the air beside a helicopter propeller.

Where are the windows? All we see are mirrors. There are an awful lot of them in this airport.

That's idiotic. Windows can't just turn themselves into mirrors. They are made of an entirely different substance, we think.

Thanks so much for telling us about molten aluminum and silver, smart guy. But how did either of those things get on the back of the windows? Don't tell us a volcano erupted in the area.

No, we're not going to move out of your way, not until you answer all of our questions. We don't care if a disgruntled customer is trying to smash a "window" with a fire extinguisher. We are almost to that point of disgruntlement, but not yet. Still, we applaud his take-charge attitude and plan to assist him by holding you back.

Success . . . we are thrilled for him.

Why is there another mirror behind the broken one?

We asked you a question, not for your impersonation of a terrified baboon.

Hey, you might want to look behind you. There's a parade of all your hopes, dreams, disappointments, embarrassments, successes, and temper tantrums. They are all coming towards you, waving knives at your throat.

Look behind you.

Never mind, we took our own advice. There is nothing behind you except a roomful of disgruntled customers.

Wait . . . your parade is marching inside the mirror. The first float rolls closer and closer.

Now we see it, now we don't. Watch your back.

That's disgusting. Can you go somewhere else? We're all trying to maintain a functional digestive system. We didn't pay good money to see viscera pour out of your body.

Oh, look what you've done now—you're dead and we feel guilty about wanting to murder you. You will always be remembered in our hearts. You were a very good person.

Saying nice things about you isn't making us feel good about ourselves. We will try another technique. We will pretend a living person still exists inside the black shape that has enveloped your body. You haven't given us any other choice. We so enjoy talking to you. We will talk until our parades come to take us away, leaving behind shadows where there once was light.

THE ADVENTURES OF A SMALL, CERAMIC GIRAFFE IN TUDOR ENGLAND

for Kek-w

A small, ceramic giraffe goes outside to buy dish soup. Outside is Tudor England. Inside is a room with a high ceiling. The giraffe does not like the high ceiling. It intimidates him. The ceiling says, "My height is wasted on you, small, ceramic giraffe." Outside, Tudor England says, "I love you, small, ceramic giraffe." But the small, ceramic giraffe cannot reciprocate this love. The giraffe does not even know Tudor England exists. How should he know? He has never seen Showtime's original series, *The Tudors*. He does not know what Tudor England looks like. When the giraffe looks at Tudor England, all he sees is a junkyard. Having never seen *The Tudors*, the small, ceramic giraffe walks to the shop as loneliness and insignificance drips down his small neck.

FOUR ANSWERS
TO FOUR QUESTIONS

1

You say: The weather is so nice. It is so nice. Don't you see how nice it is? Fishermen have cut holes into clouds, dropped their lines of sunlight to Earth. I am caught by a lure. A fisherman is reeling me towards you, to the point on the horizon where people share joy with others and talk about how the weather is nice.

The man stares. His clothes are made of mirror. You see your fist pulling intestine out of your stomach, tying it around the man's reflective sleeve. You see yourself becoming an intestinal-rope walker. The man glistens.

2

I wrap my arms around you. My fingertips into your spine, biceps fuse with your sides. Years pass. My bones become your bones, become ours. We frighten children while grocery shopping, get a monthly check from the government for being too gruesome to hold a job. We are inseparable until the grave.

3

When you turn out the light, a beam of image projects over my face, my body. It is a fractal of each member of the species considered "your type." The image conceals my flaws, your criticisms and previous hesitancies. I sleep, unaware I have become a screen for what you have left behind.

4

I left a thousand page book called I Can Do So Much Better on your bedside table. I wrote it myself. It is the only copy in existence. You turn to the first page and read:

Because you flare your nostrils when you're lying, because you flare your nostrils a lot, because you take shits after showering and forget to towel off your ass, because I taste chemicals when you kiss me, because you need to shave your unibrow four times a year, because you lose the remote control in the refrigerator, because you leave empty orange juice containers inside it, because with each breath you demand something I cannot give.

THE LUNCH DATE

Adolf Hitler tells me that I look beautiful. This unsettles me. I do not believe him. I feel like he is flattering me so I'll agree to swallow his racially pure sperm cells.

I bite down on tonight's main course. It is juicy. It is Adolf Hitler's eyeball. It tastes like nasal decongestant. I try to stop myself from gagging. I try to stop myself from gagging while Adolf Hitler bites down on his other eyeball.

I vomit Adolf Hitler's chewed eyeball back into the serving tray. I am afraid of offending him and getting sent back to the camps, so I conceal my BLAAAAGH by pressing a button that detonates a nuclear missile over Adolf Hitler's outdoor patio.

We sit calmly in our garden chairs, flesh melting off our bodies.

Adolf Hitler asks, "Vill you pass the vine?"

I don't know how much longer I can listen to Adolf Hitler's bad German accent without getting really really annoyed. And Adolf Hitler wouldn't like me when I'm really really annoyed. I hurt people's feelings when I'm really really annoyed. I say mean things like, "Hey, Adolf Hitler! Why is your stupid face so stupid looking?"

And . . .

"Hey, Adolf Hitler. Your mom's so Jewish that she worries incessantly about your health."

And . . .

"Hey, Adolf Hitler. Your Hitler mustache looks even worse now that you're a living skeleton."

But I don't say any of these things. I am only a little annoyed at Adolf Hitler's bad German rather than really really annoyed. So I say, "Of course I'll pass you the wine, Adolf Hitler, sexual dynamo. Please don't send me back to the camps."

I pass Adolf Hitler the jug of wine. My nose slides off and falls into it. Adolf Hitler grabs the jug out of my hands and drinks before I can warn him about my severed schnozzle. Adolf Hitler is now choking. I do not want Adolf Hitler to die.

I secretly love Adolf Hitler. I secretly love Adolf Hitler and I don't care what you think. If I had to choose one person to pump Zyklon B gas through my elegant dual shower head, it would be Adolf Hitler. I would clutch my throat knowing that Adolf Hitler loved me, knowing that he cared.

Adolf Hitler gasps for air. I stop visualizing the wedding dress that I'm going to wear on top of our wedding cake and go all Heimlich Maneuver over Adolf Hitler's ass.

It is very sensual.

My nose flies out of Adolf Hitler's mouth. It lands on Adolf Hitler's trampoline. The trampoline lifts it up into the sky. My nose falls down through blood-covered clouds. It lands in Adolf Hitler's mouth. Adolf Hitler is now choking.

Heimlich Maneuver. Sensuality. Trampoline. Sky. Clouds. Adolf Hitler is now choking.

Heimlich Maneuver. Sensuality. Trampoline. Sky. Clouds. Adolf Hitler is now choking.

Heimlich Maneuver. Sensuality. Trampoline. Sky. Clouds. Adolf Hitler is now choking.

And our lunch date never ends. While I give Adolf Hitler a perpetual Heimlich Maneuver, we marry, grow old together, and move to Boca Raton to spend our retirement. Eventually, Adolf Hitler is murdered by a mob of senior citizens.

TIME TO EAT

The clocks sizzle in the boiling sun. The man is cooking breakfast. He is unaware that the clocks are being overcooked. Their texture will be runny. The man's day will be ruined. He will have no time to do his errands and enjoy the pleasures of his free time. It is 8 AM but now the sun will set in ten minutes, resulting in night and extreme cold. He is not prepared for this cold. One of his errands was to buy a coat and a warm blanket. The man uses a spatula to remove one of the clocks and takes a bite. He says, "Ick!" Ten minutes pass and the day turns to night.

THE GHOST PARADE

The ghost parade felt angry because the writer was supposed to write a story about it. The ghost parade marched through the writer's bedroom. The writer woke up. He was very afraid. A ghost parade was marching through his bedroom. He called the ghost parade busters, but the ghost parade busters did not answer the phone. The writer was existing in the wrong movie. The writer told the ghost parade to march out of his bedroom. But the ghost parade did not listen to the writer. The ghost parade continued to march in his bedroom. The writer called out for his cat. The writer's cat trotted through the door. The writer told his cat about his predicament. The cat invented a machine that was supposed to scare away ghost parades. The cat turned the machine on. The machine shot screaming infant projectiles at the ghost parade. The ghost parade was really scared. The ghost parade marched out of the writer's bedroom and into his bathroom. The writer was glad he didn't have to urinate. The writer went back to sleep. His cat filled out a patent for the machine that was supposed to scare away ghost parades. The cat became a multimillionaire. He wanted to share his wealth with the writer, but the writer was asleep. Now the writer and his cat belong to different economic classes. They are ok with this.

THE STUDY

A secret passage will open if you remove a book called *Cellular Metabolism at Fifty Degrees Celsius*. The designer of the library thought no one would want to read a book that sounded so boring. The designer of the library has not been inside the study. He has never been inside anywhere. He loves nature. The secret passage leads into a woman's womb. After a secret passage seeker is ready to leave the woman's womb, he will exit the womb. The exit of the womb is located in a place that is different from the study. It is a place where the secret passage seeker has always wanted to live. The location of the place is different for each secret passage seeker. When a secret passage seeker enters a secret passage, they choose to leave a place they dislike for a place they assume they will like. But there is no returning to the old place if they don't like the new. There is no book called *Cellular Metabolism at Fifty Degrees Celsius* in the new place. There are no books there that open secret passages.

A TEXAS COWBOY AND HIS PAL, THE GENIE, ON VACATION

for Micah Malmstrom

Bermuda is nice this time of year. A Texas cowboy doesn't like it as much as his pal, The Genie, because he refuses to take off his Stetson hat. Underneath his Stetson hat, synchronized swimmers synchronize stab him in the head with toothpicks. The Genie giggles each time the Texas cowboy yelps. The Genie is cruel. The Genie staples men's hands to the ceiling whenever they omit the The in her name. The Genie is not a good pal. The Genie is a false pal. The Genie has forced the Texas cowboy into paldom. The Genie has locked the Texas cowboy in the world and hidden the key on a keychain with all the keys in the world. The Genie shouts into the Texas cowboy's ear. She says, "Let's go out tonight! Let's sunbathe tomorrow! Let's drink piña coladas out of pine cones!" But the Texas cowboy does not want to go out. The Texas cowboy does not want to sunbathe. The Texas cowboy does not want to drink piña coladas out of pine cones. The only thing the Texas cowboy wants to do is lie underneath the covers in their hotel room and try to unlock the world with the infinite keychain. The Genie hopes he will find the correct key. She is afraid of leaving the hotel room by herself. She is afraid her dreams will collapse onto themselves and turn themselves inside out and get flattened by a herd of wild buffalo and become a Twister mat for the morbidly obese.

THE ARCHITECTS OF THE DISMANTLING

for J.A. Tyler

The Earth is scheduled for dismantling at 8 AM on Monday. The architects spend a lot of time preparing for 8 AM on Monday. Their blueprints are comprehensive. Their blueprints are beautiful. The architects make a lot of sacrifices to produce blueprints that are comprehensive and beautiful. They sacrifice meals, sleep, organized work spaces, family time, grooming habits, and clock-watching activities. Without clock-watching activities, they deny themselves the pleasure of counting the ticks until the end of the world. The architects are looking forward to the dismantling. They will finally have enough time to do all the things that need to get done.

ARCHEOLOGIST

I can feel the walls closing in, feel their primitive technologies driving them to invade my personal space, sharpening their death-inducing spikes, weeping over my nuclear microwave and emotion-suppressing spike I throw into a pit of ravenous gators, shoot a grappling hook at the ceiling and knock a hole into it with a puncher, lift myself to the next floor . . . young, clean, community college, fedora-wearing, telemarketing investment banker type banana helps me up. I am evidently its idea of a lucrative financial opportunity.

The amateur archeologist wants to come on hip . . . Talks about "golden idols" and gets high off curses now and then, and keeps some around to offer the fast racecar driver types.

"Thanks, chiquita," I say, "I can see you're one of us." Its peel lights up like a self-immolating monk.

"Never liked walls much. Always getting in my way. The ones down there are due for a metamucil shot.

"Ever see a metamucil shot, chiquita? I saw The Tarzan Kid catch one in Liberia. We trapped him in the monkey house and charged a pouch of Hannukah gelt to watch it. Cut with metamucil and the junk is too gooey to be cooked with anything but a nuclear microwave. That's why I like to carry one on my head. The Tarzan Kid didn't have the financial means. Tried to shoot up the goo but his rig looked like a sticky foot. His veins weren't having it. Had to vacuum the China White with his nose. Stopped to pick the goobers out every two seconds. The zoo visitors pointed and laughed at the disgusting habit. He shot diarrhea out of his sinuses for two weeks. Passed the time by carrying a monkey on his back and trying to suicide himself with vines. Only succeeded at swinging back and forth across the enclosure. Probably cursed the day he aaaaa-aaaa-aaaa-aaa-ed into my ear wishing he was high enough to know better.

"Recollect when I am traveling with Complainer, worst fella to get stuck with in the galaxy. We is working the artifacts at a Mayan ruin. One night he turns to me and says: 'I can feel the walls closing in, feel their primitive technologies driving them to invade my personal space . . . Hated that the first time I read it. But the only other stories I could get my mitts on made my brain drip in ennui. So I read it again. And again. And again. Still hated it. But there was something about it. Something that kept me coming back. To give it another chance. Twenty times in and I loved it. Felt like it was written especially for me. Was nonsense before but it made more sense than any other story. Over ten years later and I read it again. Felt like I was reading it for the first time. Felt like I was our pal The Rube. Like the I can feel the walls closing in guy was pulling a con. I yanked the wool out of my eyes. Smelled like it hadn't been washed in a decade plus.'

"So I says: 'Since when you concerned with personal hygiene?'

"He just looks at me and says: 'Fill your hand stranger' and yanks a rocket launcher out of his anus and I hightailed it out of there, rockets decimating the walls of history. And he goes to a cafe and sends his meal back 47 times before the fuzz nail him. I mean the Complainer earned his moniker.

"Ever notice how much slang carries over from archeologists to women's studies professors? Like 'boopiting,' letting someone inject your eye yolk into their iris.

"Stomp on him!

"Stomp the Lethological Kid giving that mark the scalp shine.

"Smooth Operator whittling him down to the skull.

"The Cherubic Kid say: 'Once I swiped The Screecher's commemorative spoonful and threw it in a pot of boiling water. He didn't want to waste the shot. Gave his spike a helping of the boiling water. Only thing it did was turn his insides al dente. Went back for seconds. And thirds. Kept sending the plunger down towards his veins over the next couple o' months. Water level in the pot went down slowly. Organs turned to rancid pasta. Got bored with his arm and gave his foot a turn. Hit something vital to his walking capabilities. Had to hobble on one leg to the stove. Didn't even realize he was junk sick the whole time. Called it my spaghetti cure. Sold it to Doctor Benway. Walked in while he was shredding evidence. Made him jumpy. Accidentally cut a few strips outta his patient's brain. Interested in what would happen if he stitched them back in the wrong place. Patient woke up thinking he was a panda ice cream spatula. A life altering experience that.'

"Well," I said, tapping the hieroglyphics, "duty calls. As one loathsome specimen said to another: 'Don't do anything I wouldn't do except repeat my advice over and over again til it loses all meaning.'"

I hear a rumble and shimmy to the side of the chamber. A giant boulder makes a pancake out of the banana as the fruit pretends hideous laughter.

Swell. One less ripe imposter to get between me and my prize: a ceramic pot. The swellest ceramic pot on this scorched planet. I'm always telling Igor at the hock shop: 'Don't pay me in money. I can't shoot money.' If the legends are true, I'll never have to see his pox-ridden face again. They say the temple's ceramic pot contains a limitless supply of H. I could give up thieving and live it up in Morocco. Maybe settle down with an Arab boy named Kiki. Sell a bundle or two to pay for a white picket fence.

Goddamn. Wish I hadn't stepped on that stone. Goddamn. Bug-eyed creature pops outta a basket: "It's a trap!" Watch the stone descend, looking like a primitive elevator for holy rats. Makes a sound like polished slabs of concrete scraping against each other. I hear it in my nightmares. A Mugwump statue shoots a legion of arrows into my chest. Hope I can find the ceramic pot before I need to scream . . . nope.

CATERPILLARS AND WATERMELONS

for Mike Barrett

Caterpillars ponder watermelons. Watermelons kiss caterpillars. Caterpillars pour petrol over watermelons. Watermelons get to second base with caterpillars. Caterpillars immolate watermelons. Watermelons resurrect on the third day. Caterpillars penetrate through watermelons. Watermelons propose to caterpillars. Caterpillars eat watermelons. Watermelons digest inside caterpillars. Caterpillars excrete watermelons. Watermelons point shotguns at caterpillars. Caterpillars marry watermelons. Watermelons crush caterpillars' hopes and dreams.

A HEADLESS MAN FALLS IN LOVE WITH A BOWL OF RICE

for Nathan Tyree

The headless man is eating dinner. He feels his life is incomplete. His tears dribble out of his neck wound and major organs rain down on a bowl of rice. If the rest of his organs rain down on the bowl of rice, the headless man will stop feeling his life is incomplete. He does not want this. The only way to save himself is to make his life complete in a different way. He must use a method of hunting and trapping the missing piece rather than not feeling anything at all. The headless man has determined the missing piece is an emotion. An emotion that has been reserved for a person who is not the headless man. An emotion that will fit into his soft tissue. But where will he hunt and trap this emotion? Women are repulsed by his incompleteness, men are likely to react to it with violence. He contemplates this conundrum. He stops contemplating. He looks down at the bowl of rice with longing. He looks down at the bowl of rice, regretting all the pieces he has left behind.

THE TIME TRAVELING GIRAFFE DEFIES GOD

The time traveling giraffe has had enough. His head hurts from hitting the ceiling too many times. He opens his mouth and swallows himself. A time traveling giraffe from another time opens his mouth and regurgitates the time traveling giraffe with the sore head. God shapes Zimbabwe with his fists. The time traveling giraffe taps him on the shoulder with his paw. He says, "Excuse me, sir. Can you please give giraffes shorter necks and pogo sticks? It would make me happy." God shakes his head. The time traveling giraffe is angry. He bites off God's ear. God continues to shape Zimbabwe. The time traveling giraffe continues to suffer head pain.

IN THE RESTAURANT

The waiter brings you the most delicious lasagna known to man. Baked with all your favorite foods. Served on a supernatural plate. Pulsating with energy rendering this eclectic clash mouthwatering rather than stomach-churning.

You transport a forkful to the bottom of your nose. The aroma makes your nostril hairs tingle. You take a whiff. It reminds you of picnicking with your sweetheart on a summer day. You prepare yourself for the first nibble.

An entrée from another table catches your eye. It is an octopus smothered in mayonnaise. A glob of drool skids down your chin. You drop your fork, startled by the affection you feel for this unpalatable meal.

You stare down at the lasagna with regret. You contemplate signaling for the waiter. Instead, you choose to avoid confrontation.

A baby wails. You look over at the bane of the restaurant and film industries. It is lying inside a cradle. The cradle has been placed on top of a table between a young couple. You wonder if the restaurant is out of high chairs. Are they going to eat the baby?

You scan through the restaurant's menu. "Baby" is listed

under entrees. $26.99.

The lasagna makes a noise. It sounds like it's passing gas. You shout, "I'll have the baby if you don't. . . ." then squeeze your throat violently. No one reacts to your outburst.

A toad gasps for air. It is dying from lung cancer. You turn to give it your sympathy.

The false toad has deceived you. It is not a toad, but a shish kebab of human hearts. The hearts are working in tandem to gasp like a lung cancer patient. A man points the skewer towards his mouth. You envy him.

The aroma of the lasagna nauseates you. The supernatural plate is now powerless. Its warranty has expired.

You hurl the meal across the room. Pasta and all your favorite foods rain down upon the customers.

They react to your outburst with outbursts of their own.

You make a scary face and charge.

And after you're finished, not one iota of flesh is left on a bone.

GATHERED
IN NERDY CONGRESS

for Mitt Roj

The United States Congress is meeting for an emergency session. The emergency session involves Nintendo's decision to bribe the congressmen with Wii consoles in hopes of avoiding blame after their consoles declare war on humanity. The congressmen have brought their Wii consoles along with them. They cannot stop playing. They are not concerned with the consoles' future war on humanity. They are not aware of its inevitability. Instead, they are concerned with their inability to stop playing Wii consoles. They are ashamed of what they have become. They decide to petition Nintendo to create a country they can govern without turning off their Wii consoles. Nintendo agrees to their terms. They create a game called America 2. It is not available in stores. It is not available to the general public. You must be a United States congressman to purchase it. The congressmen like America 2 a lot. It becomes their favorite game. War begins, but it is not the congressmen's war. War begins, but it does not take place between the congressmen's borders.

THE LAUNDRY ROOM

The couple are trying to sell their house. The real estate ad lists four bedrooms. But there are only three bedrooms. The couple are trying to pass off the laundry room as a fourth bedroom. But it is not a bedroom. It is a laundry room. It is dark and dank and there is a crawlspace behind the dryer. But it is carpeted, the couple thinks, so why couldn't it be a bedroom? You can just take out the washing machine and the dryer and pretend there isn't a crawlspace and put in a bed and you'd be set.

A realtor shows the room to a potential buyer. The man says, "This is not a bedroom. This is a laundry room." The realtor says, "Look closer. This is a bedroom." The potential buyer looks behind the dryer. He gets down on his hands and knees. He crawls into the crawlspace. He looks for the bedroom. He crawls. He crawls for the next thirty years. His body hits a wall at the end of the crawlspace and he suffers a brain aneurysm. The couple never sell their house. They probably shouldn't have listed the extra bedroom.

CRAWLING OVER FIFTY GOOD PUSSIES TO GET ONE FAT BOY'S ASSHOLE

A robotic voice oozes out of the speakers: "Welcome to the Hall of Game Show Hosts, Zanyland's least popular but most distinguished attraction."

Insomniacs watch in awe as audio-animatrons flood the stage to recite catch phrases. Snores of relief drown out culturally significant phrases like, "Come on down! You're the next contestant on the Price is Right!" and "Spin That Wheel!" Finally cured, the former insomniacs are too incapacitated to complain about the historical inaccuracies of the phrases. Too comatose to yammer about how the phrases were originally spoken by the game show's announcer or a techno pop MC.

The Alex Trebek animatron straightens his holographic tie and says, "And now, here is the host of Jeopardy, Alex—"

Alex Tron's culturally significant but historically inaccurate phrase is interrupted by the sound of a machine gun. The sound of a machine gun is interrupted by an explosion.

The animatrons short circuit. They stop telling bad jokes and stand stiffly, their lips frozen into fake smiles. The lack of boredom wakes the sleepers. They demand their money back. There is no one around to give them their money back. They grind their teeth in frustration.

The short circuit has altered Alex Tron's programming. His suit morphs into an Oakland Raider's hoody and a pair of Phat Farm brand jeans that are falling down around his ankles. Then his penny loafers morph into Adidas high tops and his hair piece morphs into a doo rag. "I'm sorry," he says, "but the correct question is 'What is busting a cap in your ass?'"

Alex Tron points his finger at Chuck Woolery and pretends to bust a cap in his ass. The Chuck Woolery animatron does not try to dodge the imaginary bullet. He does not do anything. He remains stiff like all of the other game show hosts besides Alex Tron, who is doing a funny walk down off the stage as if he's moving his body to an imaginary, repetitive beat.

Alex Tron has a hell of an imagination for someone who wasn't programmed to possess one.

"My nigga," he says repeatedly as he tries to high five each of the insomniacs. But the insomniacs are too quick for him and he ends up high fiving the dust mites floating in the air.

"Why ya'all be trippin?" he asks.

The insomniacs ignore him and stare at the stage, waiting for the show and their dreams to resume.

Depressed, he walks out the exit and escapes from the Hall of Game Show Hosts forever.

Alex Tron's eyes spark as his tears fall upon the streets of Zanyland. The pavement is so clean you can eat a meal off it.

A large black man with a machine gun is eating a meal off it. It is not the kind of meal usually eaten in the year 3032. The large black man is eating another man's tongue. He seems to be enjoying it. This can be inferred by the smacking sounds he is making with his lips.

Alex Tron sees a flash of the large black man's black skin through his tears. This makes him very happy. He stops crying. He had never seen a black man before. They are not allowed in the park. The Zany board of directors are afraid they will turn the park into a garbage can with their watermelon seeds and fried chicken bones. Alex Tron thinks to himself, I wish I belonged to this alien species instead of the Alex Trebek species.

He admires the large black man's clothes. The man is wearing the garb of the late nineteenth century. Alex Tron is envious of his Stetson hat. Alex Tron is jealous of his antique fanny pack. "My nigga," he says, trying to give him a high five. The large black man stabs Alex Tron's hand with a meat cleaver. This pleases Alex Tron. Ordinarily, someone who has a meat cleaver stuck through their hand would not be pleased by this turn of events. But the Wacky imagineers have made Alex Tron indestructible and resistant to pain, so this pleases him. He says, "My nigga," and raises his other hand for another high five.

The large black man shrugs his shoulders, yanks back his meat cleaver, and goes back to his meal.

Alex Tron asks the large black man for his name.

He responds, "I'm that bad motherfucker called Stagger Lee."

Alex Tron flashes a gang sign. It looks more like an angry variation of The Itsy Bitsy Spider. He begins to rap: "My name is A-Dawg, I got a cat with a thirteen inch gat. Best not fuck with this or you'll be fucking with some motherfucking gangsta shit. I'll pull down my pants, make my pussy do a dance, and shoot a blast up your motherfucking ass." He shoots an imaginary AK-47 into the air. "Can I get an amen?"

Alex Tron does not get an amen. Stagger Lee does not

give him an amen. Stagger Lee stomped away while Alex Tron was flashing his excessively long gang sign. Stagger Lee is terrorizing Zanyland's Snack Shack. Stagger Lee is slicing off a cashier's ear.

Alex Tron goes inside the Snack Shack.

"Give me my ear back," the Snack Shack cashier says, "or I'll be seeing you in small claims court."

These are the last words the Snack Shack cashier says before Stagger Lee lifts up the cash register and introduces it to his head.

This is the verbal exchange that transpires:

Cash Register: May I burst your brains all over the counter?

Head: Why of course, my good fellow.

Now that the introductions are out of the way, Stagger Lee waves his machine gun as if he were conducting an orchestra. Bullets spray across the room.

The Snack Shack's customers disapprove of his performance. They boo. They hiss. They fling severed organs at his vintage coat. They stop breathing in protest of his cacophonic symphony.

Alex Tron celebrates Stagger Lee's atrocities with a "the roof, the roof, the roof is on fire!"

Stagger Lee looks up at the roof. It is not on fire.

Stagger Lee is perplexed.

Alex Tron picks bullet shells out of his mustache. "We don't need no water, let the mother fucker burn!"

Stagger Lee tries to clear up his confusion with another hail of bullets.

Alex Tron mistakes the bullets for chronic pellets. He swallows them. He uses oxygen to chase them down. He anxiously awaits the effect they will have on his central nervous system. He does not have a central nervous system. The imagineers did not think it was worth giving him an artificial central nervous system. The bullets have no effect on him. He thinks Stagger Lee must have given him some weak-ass shit. He does not complain because he wants Stagger Lee to like him.

The corpses in the Snack Shack make rude, gassy noises.

Alex Tron turns to admonish them: "Yo, dawgs. That's fuckin' nasty. Take a Gas-X or some shi-"

He realizes the customers are dead. This makes him upset. Alex Tron's emotional instability is beginning to fry his circuitry. His systems would be ok with one dead customer. It wouldn't even require maintenance if there were a few dead customers. But the Snack Shack is a very popular place. Alex Tron is starting to question Stagger Lee's behavior. He does this while his circuitry forces him to do jumping jacks. I am not sure if I want to convert to Stagger Lee's species if it means I will have to kill everyone in sight, he thinks. This offends my moral matrix a little.

Stagger Lee lights a cigarette and inhales the fumes. He looks cool, collected—too relaxed for someone who has just massacred a roomful of snackers. The paradox overloads Alex Tron's logic circuits, freezing his moral matrix.

Alex Tron stops crying. He stops hopscotching. He decides to breakdance upon the bodies of the dead. He makes it so.

An angry voice pipes in through the Snack Shack's speakers. The Snack Shack's speakers have never been home to an angry voice before. Previous to Stagger Lee's massacre, it had only played syrupy-sweet jingles about how corndogs are a cure for erectile dysfunction. The angry voice says, "This is Zanyland security. We are angry and contractually obligated to mention that corndogs are a cure for erectile dysfunction. We have the Snack Shack surrounded, Negroid. Put your weapons down and come out with your pants around your ankles."

Stagger Lee goes around to each table, collecting dead babies. He puts the babies on the table. He hollows out their skulls. He puts explosives where their brains used to be. He sets them to explode at the same time. One by one, he tosses the babies through the front of the Snack Shack. He puts down his machine gun. He puts down his meat cleaver.

He comes out with his pants around his ankles.

Many security guards are holding dead babies, caressing dead babies, telling dead babies that everything will be ok.

Stagger Lee counts to ten and the dead babies become his agents of destruction. The security men go to pieces. The pieces splatter all over Stagger Lee's vintage coat. He grins. He does not seem to care about the condition of his vintage coat. Perhaps he enjoys bathing in the fluids of his enemies.

Alex Tron sighs. It is such a cool coat. Its gory condition jump-starts his moral matrix, causing him to say, "Nigga, you be trippin' wit all dis exploding dead baby shit. That's some serious fucked up shit you're doin' to your coat. Can you give me directions to another bad motherfucker who don't do all this serious fucked up shit? Peace."

Stagger Lee ignores him. He goes over to a security guard and asks for directions. Half of the guard's face has been blown off. He tries to speak. His lips flop to the ground like a glob of phlegm. He stares down at his lips in regret. He looks towards Alex Tron. He uses sign language: "Do you know sign language? I had to learn it because I have a deaf child. She will be terrified of me when I go home tonight."

Alex Tron wiggles his fingers to tell the security officer that the imagineers programmed him to use sign language for the hearing impaired.

The security guard signs that Stagger Lee arrived in a time machine. He signs that maybe Alex Tron can borrow the machine to travel to wherever Stagger Lee came from and make the acquaintance of another bad mother humper, but one who doesn't do all this seriously impolite poop. He signs that the time machine looks like a Rubik's Cube, only more futuristic.

Nearby, Stagger Lee rips the head off Gerry Giraffe, exposing the torso of the staff member that lies beneath.

An eight-year-old boy manipulates his face into a frozen scream, snaps open a cell phone, and tells his lawyer to prepare a lawsuit against Zanyland for the years of psychological trauma that will result from the knowledge that Gerry Giraffe is vulnerable to decapitation.

Stagger Lee tears out the long intestine of anyone who is unfortunate enough to be standing nearby. He swings his arms around and launches his victims into the Floridian sky.

Showgirls parachute down from a Zanyplane. They do not bat a heavily mascaraed eyelash at the mutilated bodies skyrocketing past them.

The angry voice is back again. It says, "Use these women with our compliments. Just don't hurt anyone else."

Stagger Lee looks at the parachuting showgirls and snarls, "I'll climb over fifty good pussies to get one fat boy's asshole."

Alex Tron locates Stagger Lee's time machine in a pile of gallbladders. It really does look like a Rubik's Cube. It also has bright lights that flash in different colors. This makes Alex Tron think of the future. He tries to solve the puzzle.

He cannot solve the puzzle. He wishes the imagineers had programmed him with puzzle-solving capabilities. He considers telling Stagger Lee where their office is located.

The surviving security officers form a single file line, remove their pants, bend down, and point their buttocks towards Stagger Lee.

Stagger Lee stomps over to the back of the line. The officer at the end looks frightened. Stagger Lee leers at his asshole and says, "Fuck this shit. Turn around and suck my dick or you gonna be dead."

The officer agrees with a slurp and "mmm mmm mmm" sounds.

Stagger Lee's eyes glaze over in pleasure.

Alex Tron's moral matrix is very disturbed by the mouth

rape. He cannot stop tap dancing. He tap dances over to the sexual assault. He goes through the officer's pants while tap dancing. He locates the officer's zanygun while tap dancing. He presses it to Stagger Lee's forehead while tap dancing.

Stagger Lee does not notice.

Alex Tron tap dances as he pulls the trigger and yells, "Buck buck buck buck!"

A missile escapes out of the gun barrel. It penetrates Stagger Lee's skull.

A flash of fire is seen through his ears, nose, and throat.

His glazed eyes cook in their sockets. A hole explodes through his hat. A miniature mushroom cloud rises out of it.

Blixa Bargeld lets out the illest scream that Alex Tron has ever heard.

Alex Tron stops tap dancing.

INVINCIBLE

The boy goes to the store and buys oak tag and colored pencils. He sets up a table and chair outside his house, puts a jug of his mother's lemonade down on the table, writes "lemommade 25 sents," on the piece of oak tag, tapes it to the table so its bottom faces the sidewalk and flops around in the summer breeze.

It is early in the morning. Business is slow. Hours pass. Business picks up. The street is congested with thirsty automobile owners. The boy has almost enough money to buy a kit for making refrigerator magnets. The boy really wants to make his own refrigerator magnets.

Billy and Jack come down the street in fine Italian suits. The boy does not like Billy and Jack. They are bullies. Their skin swelters in the heat. The boy thinks, "Why are they wearing such heavy clothes in the summer?"

Billy says, "One lemonade please." He flashes Jack a malignant grin.

Billy's politeness makes the boy fear him even more. He pours the lemonade into a cup. "Twe . . . twe . . . twen . . . ty fi . . . fi . . . five cen . . . cents p . . . p . . . p . . . p . . . please."

Jack removes a Tommy Gun from his pants, which contain

an interdimensional dimension transcending time and space. He pours the lemonade on the sidewalk . . . slowly. "Faggot," he says, "You're cutting into our business, faggot. Go inside and stay there, faggot, unless you wanna be filled full of holes and eaten like Swiss cheese."

The boy cries.

Billy says, "I like cheese."

Tears fall into the boy's collar. It is both uncomfortable and refreshing.

The boy's mother comes out of the house. She is screaming. She is not screaming words. She is screaming sounds.

Rata tat tat. Jack shoots the mother in the chest with his Tommy Gun.

She is not bothered by the bullets. She is unfazed.

Mothers are indestructible.

She screams some more. Cacophonic sounds.

Billy and Jack cry. They run away.

The mother picks up her grieving son and carries him inside the house.

ALLIGATOR IN SPACE

The alligator astronaut is hungry. His shuttle is floating two million light years from Earth and he wants some meat. But mission control has forgotten to pack him freeze-dried deli slices. The only things they left on the shuttle are astronaut ice cream and bread. The alligator astronaut is not fond of astronaut ice cream. He does not understand what is ice cream-y about it. It is not cold. It is not wet. The alligator astronaut thinks astronaut ice cream is what you get when you leave cotton candy in a dark basement for 100 years. So he chooses the bread and opens the bread bag. The loaf floats out of the bag and away from his grasp. He tries to do the backstroke across the room and capture the bread. But it is no use. He floats in the opposite direction. He gives up and cries tears of hunger. The tears float across the room. It is beautiful, but the alligator astronaut is not prepared to appreciate its beauty.

SCENES FROM THE LIFE OF A GREETING CARD DESIGNER

OCTOBER 31, 5008 BS

Missiles fly through Tim Hallmark's cardboard window while he puts the finishing touches on his latest creation. He loses interest in calligraphing, "I bear about you," underneath a drawing of a big bear crushing the life out of a little bear. He gains interest in the flames eating through his cardboard couch. He picks up a cardboard fire extinguisher and shoots cardboard foam at his cardboard couch. The flames grow in stature. He is ashamed of his inability to afford an aluminum extinguisher.

Outside, a little boy in a Patrick Swayze mask yells, "Give us some candy or prepare for annihilation."

Tim Hallmark grabs his cardboard AK-47, crawls over to the window, shoots cardboard bullets at the little boy and his masked posse, and yells, "Didn't you read the greeting card I stapled to the front door?"

Yes, the masked children have read the greeting card he stapled to the front door. No, they will not give their deep and heartfelt sympathies to Tim Hallmark during his time of need. No, they cannot bring themselves to forgive him for being unable to afford non-cardboard flavored Halloween candy. Children do not enjoy cardboard Halloween candy. Children enjoy cardboard Halloween candy even less when it is presented to them inside a cardboard box with "One per person PLEASE!!!" calligraphed on it. Children have been known to misbehave when presented with cardboard Halloween candy. Children have been known to misbehave on Halloween. They may obey the rules of their parents and the state on every other day of the year, but on the last few Halloweens they've become the scourge of the Earth.

Tim Hallmark loves children, but the masked children have just grenaded the cardboard roof off his cardboard house and Tim Hallmark does not love masked children who grenade his cardboard roof off his cardboard house.

Tim Hallmark looks through the hole where his roof used to be. He sees a nuclear warhead hurtling towards him. He sees an airplane, but not the little girl in a Chewbacca mask giggling in its cockpit.

Tim Hallmark watches the nuclear warhead and thinks about his life. He screams out the words from his favorite creations:

Happy birthday! You are one day closer to your putrification!

Happy Mother's Day, but I never asked to be thrust out of rotting taco!

Sorry your grandma died! She molested me when I was eight!

He doesn't understand why the American public has never understood his genius. He doesn't understand why they haven't showered him with riches. He regrets never finding true love.

Tim Hallmark is very depressed. He is very depressed and a nuclear warhead is about to disintegrate his head.

OCTOBER 31, 5009 BS

This year, Tim Hallmark saved up his money from his new part-time job as a sideshow attraction and bought poison eggplant candies in bulk. "One for you," he says to a little naked boy in a 42-foot white beard, "and one for you," he says to a little girl in a naughty nurse costume. He has been poisoning thousands of little girls and boys all night from the comfort of his dumpster. They have been complimenting him on his mask. He is very bitter about their compliments. He does not tell them that it is not a mask, that his face has been maligned by radiation poisoning. He does not want to horrify them with this factoid. He does not want them to run away. Instead, he wants them to stay put and thank him for his delicious poison eggplant candies.

The effects of the poison begin. A horde of little girls and boys stammer towards his dumpster with an amalgam of pus and blood spewing out of their orifices. "What have you done to us?" they ask.

A little boy tears opens a greeting card envelope and card, sees a picture of a skeleton in a thong bikini. Under the picture, he reads:

Roses are red
Violets are blue
You have been poisoned
and it sucks to be you.

Below the poem, he deciphers Tim Hallmark's flowery handwriting:

Help me overthrow the government if you ever want to see your mommies and daddies again. My antidote tastes like chocolate milkshake.

XOXO,

Tim Hallmark

The little poisoned girls and boys overthrow the government for Tim Hallmark. This makes him happy. He is the new dictator.

The little poisoned girls and boys are not happy. They are still spewing an amalgam of pus and blood out of their orifices. They are taking an extremely long time to die. They are in agony.

They look at Tim Hallmark as if he were a cruel man. But he is not a cruel man. The sideshow business just isn't very lucrative. It may have paid for his supply of poison eggplant candies, but it wasn't enough to afford the antidote.

"Stop looking at me like that!" Tim Hallmark says as he addresses the nation on live TV. "My first amendment to the Constitution is to send everyone who doesn't stop looking at me like that to rape camp. My second amendment to the constitution is to send everyone who doesn't buy at least one of my greeting cards a day to rape camp."

And so begins Tim Hallmark's reign as the top-selling greeting card designer in the country.

OCTOBER 31, 5010 BS

Tim Hallmark leaves the White House with an army of bodyguards. He wants to visit Fort Knox and rub his testicles over every gold bar in the treasury. He wants his testicles to feel that cold, refreshing sensation millions and millions of times.

Tim Hallmark only travels by parade float. His float rolls

towards Fort Knox. He stands in the center of a giant chocolate rose and takes a nibble whenever he gets a craving. His army of bodyguards march on the side, hoping to avoid rape camp, hoping they won't accidentally insult their dictator.

Tim Hallmark is easily insulted.

Terrorists attack Tim Hallmark's float with airplanes. Many bodyguards save Tim Hallmark's life by blocking the crashing planes with their bodies.

By doing this, they avoid rape camp. Getting hit by an airplane is preferable to rape camp.

Tim Hallmark does not negotiate with terrorists.

Terrorists = the parents of the children he poisoned last Halloween.

Tim Hallmark arrives at Fort Knox. He goes inside, leaving his bodyguards behind. There are too many to fit inside the lobby. All of the bodyguards or none of the bodyguards— this is the principle that Tim Hallmark's dictatorship is based upon.

Fort Knox's lobby looks like the inside of a savings bank. He does not think this is peculiar. He is too busy leering at the teller's exquisite beauty. He wants to have sex with her. He will have sex with her. He is the dictator and no one wants to go to rape camp.

He cuts the line and hands the teller a greeting card. She opens it. It shows a newborn baby holding a human heart as if it were a rattle and reads, "Will you be my Valentine?"

The teller looks horrified. She looks a little less exquisitely beautiful. Tim Hallmark is ok with this. He winks at her and says, "You're too beautiful for rape camp but just right for my collection of camel skin condoms." He feels a little sad. He knows his tryst with the bank teller will be identical to the thousands of empty sexual experiences that have come before. He is beginning to think saying, "You're too beautiful for rape camp but just right for my collection of camel skin condoms," isn't the best way to start a meaningful relationship. But maybe this time it'll be different and he'll find true love. Feel something warm and fuzzy in his head rather than just something warm and gooey down below.

The teller tries to stop looking horrified. She says, "Follow me to the vault, Mr. Dictator."

She leads him into an enormous room. It is empty.

Tim Hallmark asks, "Where are my gold bars? Where is your golden lingerie? Where is my true love?"

The teller transforms into a tank. The tank shoots Tim Hallmark in the crotch with an armor-piercing kinetic energy penetrator.

Tim Hallmark is very stupid for being tricked into believing Fort Knox is run by a bunch of bankers instead of the U.S. Army and their killer robots.

OCTOBER 31, 5011 BS

Tim Hallmark is not the dictator anymore. He is an exile and a eunuch. He hides in the sewers because the parents of the children he poisoned two Halloweens ago are still trying to work out their grief with acts of violence and he no longer has an army of bodyguards to threaten with rape camp.

The sewers are awash in greeting cards. Tim Hallmark has been very productive since journeying down below. Right now, he is sitting on a pipe, working on his latest creation. He is calligraphing the words, "I'll never flush you, my darling. We're purr-fect for each other." He has already drawn a cat blowing kisses at an unflushed bowel movement. All of his soggy greeting cards have been designed for bowel movement and urine recipients. Tim Hallmark does not care if bowel movements and urine cannot read. Tim Hallmark does not care if bowel movements and urine lack the sentiency to be classified as recipients. Tim Hallmark doesn't have anyone else to make greeting cards for besides rats and alligators, and Tim

Hallmark is no friend of rats and alligators.

A little boy in a black person's mask rises out of the sewage, holding a Super Soaker. He says, "Give us some candy or prepare for annihilation."

Many little girls and boys in masks representing various ethnic groups emerge out of the sewage.

Tim Hallmark asks, "Didn't I kill all the little girls and boys?"

The little girls and boys say, "Yes, but that was when we were babies. Now we're all grown up and you must give us some candy or we will annihilate you."

Tim Hallmark says, "I don't have to buy Halloween candy anymore. I live in the sewers. Little girls and boys do not live in the sewers." He stares at them in terror. "Little girls and boys should not be in the sewers. I should not have to avoid annihilation by buying candy!"

The little girls and boys say, "We tracked you to the sewers to avenge the deaths of our older brothers and sisters. We would also be happy with a bunch of candy."

Tim Hallmark is nervous. He twitches. The little girls and boys aim their Super Soakers at his head. He realizes the Super Soakers are just water guns. He wonders why the manufacturers designed them to resemble bazookas. He stops twitching. He starts to cackle. He says, "What? Are you going to soak me to death?"

The little girls and boys do not say anything. They press the triggers on their Super Soakers. Flames shoot out. Tim Hallmark is on fire.

Tim Hallmark considers jumping into the sewage. He hesitates. That is where the little girls and boys are standing. He does not want them to shoot more fire at him. He does not want to be engulfed in twice as many flames.

The little girls and boys say, "Now we're going to put you out because we like you . . . Our older brothers and sisters were really mean." They each press a button on their Super Soakers and pull the trigger. The guns now shoot water. Tim Hallmark is not on fire anymore. The little girls and boys say, "Give us some candy or prepare for a second round of annihilation."

Tim Hallmark says, "Ok." He pretends to look for candy. He is actually looking for dry greeting cards. He is actually folding them into origami shuriken.

He kills all the little girls and boys with his origami shuriken.

Tim Hallmark is ninja.

He does a little dance to celebrate being ninja. He notices his reflection in the sewage. He falls in love with it. This love is a by-product of not being in the presence of a woman since last Halloween. This love wouldn't have been possible without the help of the armor-piercing kinetic energy penetrator that evaporated his crotch. He is not sexually attracted to his reflection. He is spiritually attracted to his reflection. He lacks the capacity for sexual attraction, but not spiritual attraction. He has found true love.

He takes out a piece of cardstock, draws Cupid with a bow and arrow in his mouth, calligraphies, "I'll love you until your flesh rots off your skeleton," puts the card in an envelope, gives it to himself, says, "Thank you."

Then he takes off his scalp and prepares for spiritual penetration.

DEFEAT OF
THE MOUNTAIN SPIRIT

Mount Holyoke packs a thermos and trail mix for its hike up Bradley Sands. Mount Holyoke gets up early in the morning to avoid other hikers and full exposure to the summer heat. Mount Holyoke drives to the foot of Bradley Sands. Mount Holyoke is very excited about the hike. Mount Holyoke gets out of its car. Mount Holyoke looks down at Bradley Sands and whimpers. Mount Holyoke realizes a hike up Bradley Sands will only take nine-tenths of a millisecond. Mount Holyoke releases a flash flood of sadness.

ONE OF THOSE POORLY WRITTEN STORIES THAT ARE IMPOSSIBLE TO FOLLOW BECAUSE THERE ARE TOO MANY GODDAMN CHARACTERS

Grover pogo-sticked up the staircase, passing a tour group. Arthur, their guide, recited the stair's criminal history, placing particular emphasis on the time it tied a rope ladder to the subway tracks, greased its mustache, and cackled like Regis Philbin.

Jenny envied her husband's ability to use the lecture as a sleep-aid; he dreamt of a never-ending urinal deposit.

The stairs wondered if the man always slept standing up and considered giving it a try, hoping to cure its lower back pain.

Frank regretted selling his collection of witty retorts to finance this vacation and scanned his brain cells for a suitable insult to heckle the tour guide, locating only: your chest is as flat as a two-year-old dry-erase board.

But not everyone is an uncultured piglet who can't appreciate a good trip back into the annals of European history–Kamikaze Cohn was so excited by the lesson that she punctured through the twenty-third step with the concrete Dolce & Gabbana shoe her mob boss dad gave her for her sweet sixteen, which sent a shockwave of destruction up and down the staircase.

Stan's life flashed before his eyes, which mostly consisted of waiting on the couch for someone on TV to get decapitated by a ball.

Sharon was a bit bored by the feature presentation, so she found solace in a box of Sno-Caps and was overjoyed that for once she hadn't finished the nonpareils before the end of the trailers.

Then Grover hopped onto the final step, and he and the climbers plunged into oblivion. . . .

HOLD-UP

Parker pulls the giant-sized fedora over his face, peeks through the eye slits in the crown, turns the safety off on his .38 Special, yanks the door open, runs inside. The cashier is watching a movie on his portable DVD player. Parker leans over the counter, touches the cashier's forehead with the tip of the .38, shouts demands. The giant-sized fedora muffles his speech. The cashier experiences confusion. He figures Parker is asking for directions to the expressway. It is difficult to locate. He's never dealt with someone who was so hard up that he expressed his frustration with a gun. He says, "Well, first you've gotta turn right onto Elm, then drive past two lights until you see a . . ." Parker pulls the trigger. Bits of skull splatter across a stack of American Spirits. Parker jumps the counter, shakes violently since he hadn't meant to pull the trigger, blames his nervous finger. He presses the NO SALE button on the register. The drawer opens. Parker can't see stacks of bills. It's too dark, shadowy. The rest of the store is bright. Parker lifts his fedora, sticks his face into the drawer for a better look. The darkness engulfs his nose. It feels numb. He lifts his chin, reaches for his nose. The center of his face feels smooth. His nose is gone. He panics, sniffs, smells vinegar. Feels an itch. Tries to scratch it.

Becomes unbearable. Tears his nails into the center of his face. Draws blood. No relief. A hundred dollar bill rips through his forehead and asks to borrow money for cigarettes. Parker does not respond. He cannot respond. His left ear does it for him: "Sorry, I'm an ear. We're always out of cash." The center of Parker's face remains silent.

THE WRITER

1

Last year, *Sleeping and Waking Up* was on *The New York Times'* bestsellers list for thirty-two consecutive weeks. The novel made the writer a lot of money. *Sleeping and Waking Up* was just the right book at just the right time. It was the time when houses were turning themselves inside out. Readers were looking for something simple to help them through the trauma. We wanted an 862 page description of a man sleeping. We wanted a 412 page description of a man waking up. We did not want any artsy-fartsy bullshit about a man dreaming.

The citizens of the United States are a simple people.

The writer had already spent all of his royalties on deviated septums and showroom dummies. He was looking for an idea for a novel that would keep a tarp over his head and his belly full of fossils.

They can hear the lotto balls in the writer's head churning next door.

They can hear the writer think, What if a man programs his VCR?

They do not pay attention to his next idea. They are too

busy looking out the window. They see an alligator driving an army.

They can hear the writer think, What if a doctor gave a man a prostate exam?

They do not pay attention to his next idea. They are too busy looking out the window. They see a gang of top hats sexually harassing a feathered boa.

They can hear the writer think, What if a baby cries during the night?

They do not pay attention to his next idea. They are too busy looking out the window. They see abominable snowmen enjoying the thrills of a water slide.

They can hear the writer think, What if a writer wakes up early in the morning to write a short story?

2

The writer had woken up early in the morning to write a short story. It was about a plumber. The plumber was having a really bad day. He could not plunge a customer's toilet. The toilet was filled with bowel movement. Bowel movement was the plumber's arch-nemesis.

The story was called "The Plumber."

The writer had woken up early to write sentences until either the plumber defeated his arch-nemesis or was defeated by his arch-nemesis.

The arch-nemesis was a very passive arch-nemesis. It did not attack. It did not threaten to take over the world. It was an ordinary bowel movement, as most bowl movements are.

The writer hoped the plumber would defeat his arch-nemesis. He also hoped the trees outside his home would stop raping his cocker spaniel. He'd been having trouble sleeping through her screams. The writer found this unacceptable. He needed his sleep. Without a good night's sleep, he found it difficult to discover whether or not various blue collar workers were able to defeat their arch-nemeses.

There is a knock on the writer's office door. The writer opens the door. The state of Virginia charges into the room.

The writer was afraid this would happen. The great state of Virginia charges into the writer's office every day, but usually not until after 9 AM. This is why the writer woke up early to write his short story.

The writer says, "Now I won't ever know if the plumber defeats his arch-nemesis." Then he removes a lasso from his desk drawer, ties a noose, puts his head in the noose, throws the other end of the lasso around the city of Richmond, and insults Virginia's virtue.

Virginia is very offended. It is very angry. It jumps up and down in an attempt to work through its rage.

The writer gasps his last breath. The plumber will have to defeat his arch-nemesis without him.

HOW TO GET BEAUTIFUL WOMEN INTO BED

It is the first day of spring, the day when the men of the village make their blood sacrifices for the upcoming year. Blood sacrifices so they'll have good luck with the women of the village. Blood sacrifices so they'll have many opportunities to fuck lots of hot chicks.

In the morning, they burn the crops and execute the cattle. After lunch, they decapitate half of the children in the village. For dessert, they rape and murder all the women between the ages of 25 and 28. Before dinner, they declare war on all the nations of the Earth. Around bedtime, they nuclear-bomb all those nations back to the ice age.

The men in the village now have the self-confidence to fuck lots of hot chicks. They do not know why this is. It's just the way things are done in this village.

ELECTRONIC GAMING NEWS

I like pausing the game
when I'm on my last life,
when a fiendish and ridiculous foe
is about to fall on my head,
when there's nowhere to run.
I like to pause the game
and watch the frozen image for hours,
delaying the inevitable.

ABOUT THE ARTIST

Sam Pink lives in Chicago, IL. He is the author of *The Self-Esteem Holocaust Comes Home* (Lazy Fascist Press), *Person* (Lazy Fascist Press), *Frowns Need Friends Too* (Afterbirth Books), and *I Am Going to Clone Myself Then Kill the Clone and Eat It* (Paperhero Press).

Visit him online at impersonalelectroniccommunication.com.

ABOUT THE AUTHOR

Bradley Sands lives in Boulder, CO, where he edits *Bust Down the Door and Eat All the Chickens*. He is the author of *My Heart Said No, But the Camera Crew Said Yes!* (Raw Dog Screaming Press), *It Came From Below the Belt* (Afterbirth Books), *Disappointing Sophomoric Effort* (forthcoming), and *TV Snorted My Brain* (forthcoming).

Visit him online at bradleysands.com.

Bizarro books

CATALOG   SPRING 2010

Bizarro Books publishes under the following imprints:

www.rawdogscreamingpress.com

www.eraserheadpress.com

www.afterbirthbooks.com

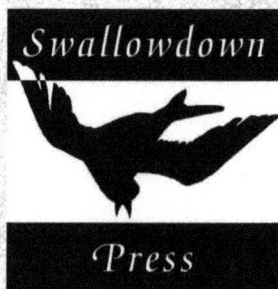

www.swallowdownpress.com

For all your Bizarro needs visit:

WWW.BIZARROCENTRAL.COM

Introduce yourselves to the bizarro genre and all of its authors with the Bizarro Starter Kit series. Each volume features short novels and short stories by ten of the leading bizarro authors, designed to give you a perfect sampling of the genre for only $5 plus shipping.

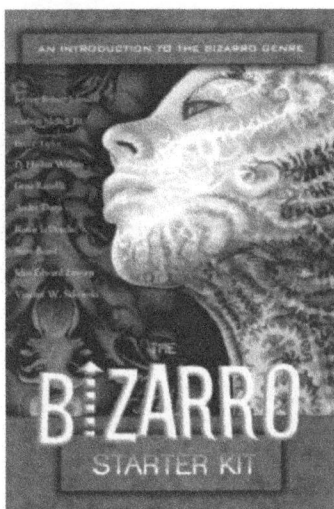

BB-0X1
"The Bizarro Starter Kit" (Orange)

Featuring D. Harlan Wilson, Carlton Mellick III, Jeremy Robert Johnson, Kevin L Donihe, Gina Ranalli, Andre Duza, Vincent W. Sakowski, Steve Beard, John Edward Lawson, and Bruce Taylor.

236 pages $5

BB-0X2
"The Bizarro Starter Kit" (Blue)

Featuring Ray Fracalossy, Jeremy C. Shipp, Jordan Krall, Mykle Hansen, Andersen Prunty, Eckhard Gerdes, Bradley Sands, Steve Aylett, Christian TeBordo, and Tony Rauch.

244 pages $5

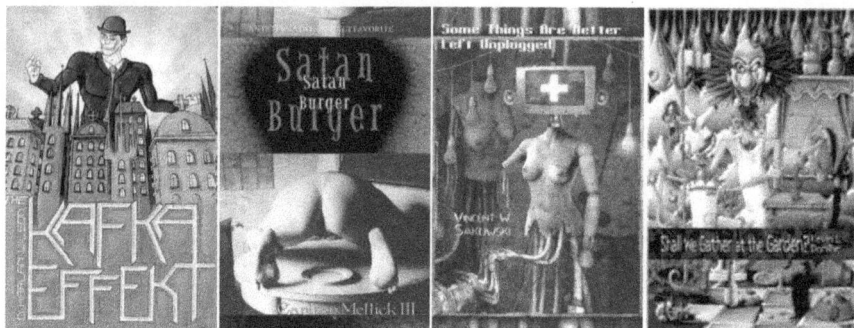

BB-001"The Kafka Effekt" D. Harlan Wilson - A collection of forty-four irreal short stories loosely written in the vein of Franz Kafka, with more than a pinch of William S. Burroughs sprinkled on top. **211 pages $14**

BB-002 "Satan Burger" Carlton Mellick III - The cult novel that put Carlton Mellick III on the map ... Six punks get jobs at a fast food restaurant owned by the devil in a city violently overpopulated by surreal alien cultures. **236 pages $14**

BB-003 "Some Things Are Better Left Unplugged" Vincent Sakwoski - Join The Man and his Nemesis, the obese tabby, for a nightmare roller coaster ride into this postmodern fantasy. **152 pages $10**

BB-004 "Shall We Gather At the Garden?" Kevin L Donihe - Donihe's Debut novel. Midgets take over the world, The Church of Lionel Richie vs. The Church of the Byrds, plant porn and more! **244 pages $14**

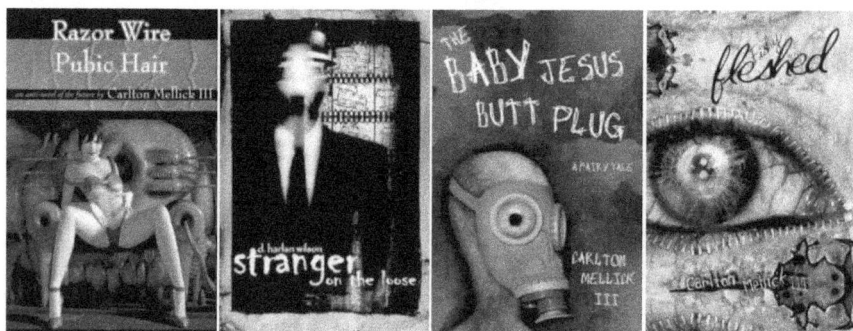

BB-005 "Razor Wire Pubic Hair" Carlton Mellick III - A genderless humandildo is purchased by a razor dominatrix and brought into her nightmarish world of bizarre sex and mutilation. **176 pages $11**

BB-006 "Stranger on the Loose" D. Harlan Wilson - The fiction of Wilson's 2nd collection is planted in the soil of normalcy, but what grows out of that soil is a dark, witty, otherworldly jungle... **228 pages $14**

BB-007 "The Baby Jesus Butt Plug" Carlton Mellick III - Using clones of the Baby Jesus for anal sex will be the hip sex fetish of the future. **92 pages $10**

BB-008 "Fishyfleshed" Carlton Mellick III - The world of the past is an illogical flatland lacking in dimension and color, a sick-scape of crispy squid people wandering the desert for no apparent reason. **260 pages $14**

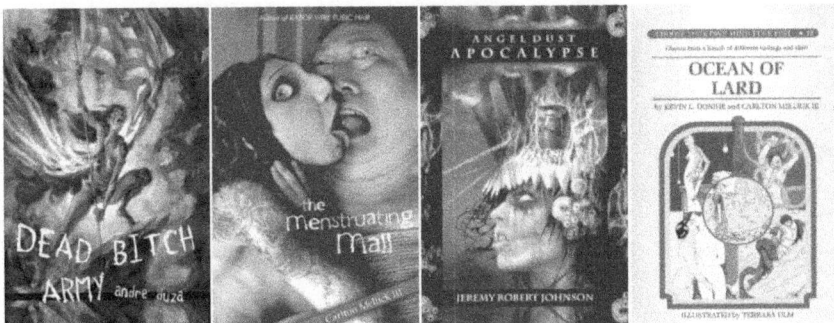

BB-009 "Dead Bitch Army" Andre Duza - Step into a world filled with racist teenagers, cannibals, 100 warped Uncle Sams, automobiles with razor-sharp teeth, living graffiti, and a pissed-off zombie bitch out for revenge. **344 pages $16**

BB-010 "The Menstruating Mall" Carlton Mellick III - "The Breakfast Club meets Chopping Mall as directed by David Lynch." - Brian Keene **212 pages $12**

BB-011 "Angel Dust Apocalypse" Jeremy Robert Johnson - Meth-heads, man-made monsters, and murderous Neo-Nazis. "Seriously amazing short stories..." - Chuck Palahniuk, author of Fight Club **184 pages $11**

BB-012 "Ocean of Lard" Kevin L Donihe / Carlton Mellick III - A parody of those old Choose Your Own Adventure kid's books about some very odd pirates sailing on a sea made of animal fat. **176 pages $12**

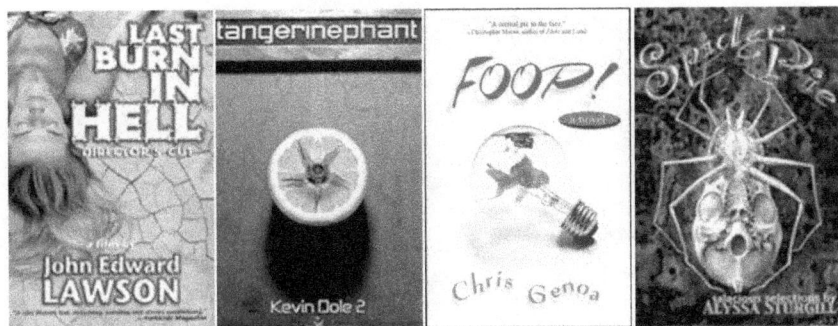

BB-013 "Last Burn in Hell" John Edward Lawson - From his lurid angst-affair with a lesbian music diva to his ascendance as unlikely pop icon the one constant for Kenrick Brimley, official state prison gigolo, is he's got no clue what he's doing. **172 pages $14**

BB-014 "Tangerinephant" Kevin Dole 2 - TV-obsessed aliens have abducted Michael Tangerinephant in this bizarre combination of science fiction, satire, and surrealism. **164 pages $11**

BB-015 "Foop!" Chris Genoa - Strange happenings are going on at Dactyl, Inc, the world's first and only time travel tourism company.

"A surreal pie in the face!" - Christopher Moore **300 pages $14**

BB-016 "Spider Pie" Alyssa Sturgill - A one-way trip down a rabbit hole inhabited by sexual deviants and friendly monsters, fairytale beginnings and hideous endings. **104 pages $11**

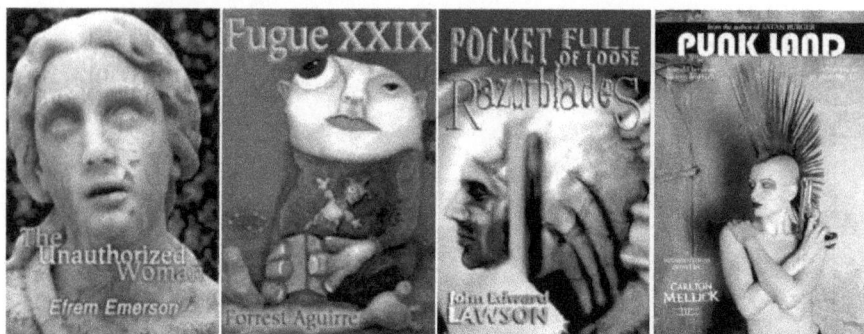

BB-017 "The Unauthorized Woman" Efrem Emerson - Enter the world of the inner freak, a landscape populated by the pre-dead and morticioners, by cockroaches and 300-lb robots. **104 pages $11**

BB-018 "Fugue XXIX" Forrest Aguirre - Tales from the fringe of speculative literary fiction where innovative minds dream up the future's uncharted territories while mining forgotten treasures of the past. **220 pages $16**

BB-019 "Pocket Full of Loose Razorblades" John Edward Lawson - A collection of dark bizarro stories. From a giant rectum to a foot-fungus factory to a girl with a biforked tongue. **190 pages $13**

BB-020 "Punk Land" Carlton Mellick III - In the punk version of Heaven, the anarchist utopia is threatened by corporate fascism and only Goblin, Mortician's sperm, and a blue-mohawked female assassin named Shark Girl can stop them. **284 pages $15**

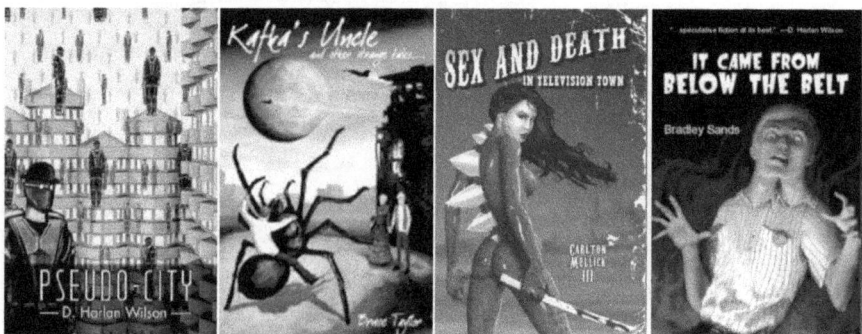

BB-021"Pseudo-City" D. Harlan Wilson - Pseudo-City exposes what waits in the bathroom stall, under the manhole cover and in the corporate boardroom, all in a way that can only be described as mind-bogglingly irreal. **220 pages $16**

BB-022 "Kafka's Uncle and Other Strange Tales" Bruce Taylor - Anslenot and his giant tarantula (tormentor? fri-end?) wander a desecrated world in this novel and collection of stories from Mr. Magic Realism Himself. **348 pages $17**

BB-023 "Sex and Death In Television Town" Carlton Mellick III - In the old west, a gang of hermaphrodite gunslingers take refuge from a demon plague in Telos: a town where its citizens have televisions instead of heads. **184 pages $12**

BB-024 "It Came From Below The Belt" Bradley Sands - What can Grover Goldstein do when his severed, sentient penis forces him to return to high school and help it win the presidential election? **204 pages $13**

BB-025 "Sick: An Anthology of Illness" John Lawson, editor - These Sick stories are horrendous and hilarious dissections of creative minds on the scalpel's edge. **296 pages $16**

BB-026 "Tempting Disaster" John Lawson, editor - A shocking and alluring anthology from the fringe that examines our culture's obsession with taboos. **260 pages $16**

BB-027 "Siren Promised" Jeremy Robert Johnson & Alan M Clark - Nominated for the Bram Stoker Award. A potent mix of bad drugs, bad dreams, brutal bad guys, and surreal/incredible art by Alan M. Clark. **190 pages $13**

BB-028 "Chemical Gardens" Gina Ranalli - Ro and punk band Green is the Enemy find Kreepkins, a surfer-dude warlock, a vengeful demon, and a Metal Priestess in their way as they try to escape an underground nightmare. **188 pages $13**

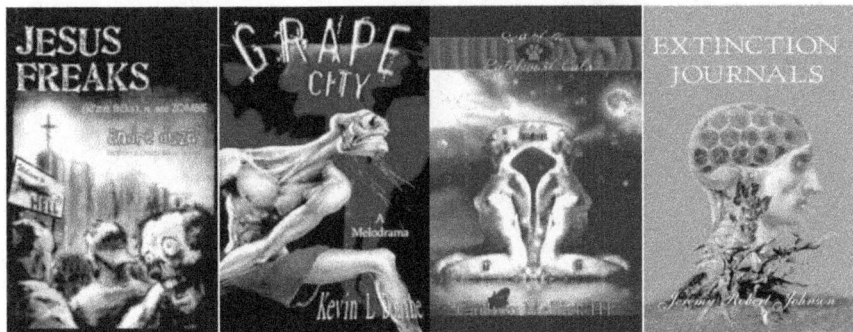

BB-029 "Jesus Freaks" Andre Duza - For God so loved the world that he gave his only two begotten sons… and a few million zombies. **400 pages $16**

BB-030 "Grape City" Kevin L. Donihe - More Donihe-style comedic bizarro about a demon named Charles who is forced to work a minimum wage job on Earth after Hell goes out of business. **108 pages $10**

BB-031"Sea of the Patchwork Cats" Carlton Mellick III - A quiet dreamlike tale set in the ashes of the human race. For Mellick enthusiasts who also adore The Twilight Zone. **112 pages $10**

BB-032 "Extinction Journals" Jeremy Robert Johnson - An uncanny voyage across a newly nuclear America where one man must confront the problems associated with loneliness, insane dieties, radiation, love, and an ever-evolving cockroach suit with a mind of its own. **104 pages $10**

BB-033 "Meat Puppet Cabaret" Steve Beard - At last! The secret connection between Jack the Ripper and Princess Diana's death revealed! **240 pages $16 / $30**

BB-034 "The Greatest Fucking Moment in Sports" Kevin L. Donihe - In the tradition of the surreal anti-sitcom Get A Life comes a tale of triumph and agape love from the master of comedic bizarro. **108 pages $10**

BB-035 "The Troublesome Amputee" John Edward Lawson - Disturbing verse from a man who truly believes nothing is sacred and intends to prove it. **104 pages $9**

BB-036 "Deity" Vic Mudd - God (who doesn't like to be called "God") comes down to a typical, suburban, Ohio family for a little vacation—but it doesn't turn out to be as relaxing as He had hoped it would be... **168 pages $12**

BB-037 "The Haunted Vagina" Carlton Mellick III - It's difficult to love a woman whose vagina is a gateway to the world of the dead. **132 pages $10**

BB-038 "Tales from the Vinegar Wasteland" Ray Fracalossy - Witness: a man is slowly losing his face, a neighbor who periodically screams out for no apparent reason, and a house with a room that doesn't actually exist. **240 pages $14**

BB-039 "Suicide Girls in the Afterlife" Gina Ranalli - After Pogue commits suicide, she unexpectedly finds herself an unwilling "guest" at a hotel in the Afterlife, where she meets a group of bizarre characters, including a goth Satan, a hippie Jesus, and an alien-human hybrid. **100 pages $9**

BB-040 "And Your Point Is?" Steve Aylett - In this follow-up to LINT multiple authors provide critical commentary and essays about Jeff Lint's mind-bending literature. **104 pages $11**

BB-041 "Not Quite One of the Boys" Vincent Sakowski - While drug-dealer Maxi drinks with Dante in purgatory, God and Satan play a little tri-level chess and do a little bargaining over his business partner, Vinnie, who is still left on earth. **220 pages $14**

BB-042 "Teeth and Tongue Landscape" Carlton Mellick III - On a planet made out of meat, a socially-obsessive monophobic man tries to find his place amongst the strange creatures and communities that he comes across. **110 pages $10**

BB-043 "War Slut" Carlton Mellick III - Part "1984," part "Waiting for Godot," and part action horror video game adaptation of John Carpenter's "The Thing." **116 pages $10**

BB-044 "All Encompassing Trip" Nicole Del Sesto - In a world where coffee is no longer available, the only television shows are reality TV re-runs, and the animals are talking back, Nikki, Amber and a singing Coyote in a do-rag are out to restore the light **308 pages $15**

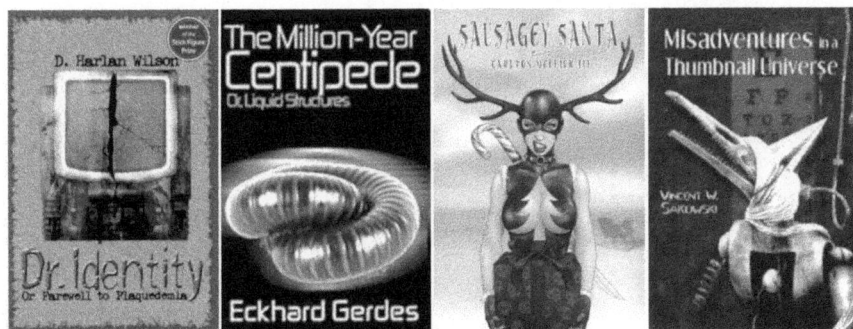

BB-045 "Dr. Identity" D. Harlan Wilson - Follow the Dystopian Duo on a killing spree of epic proportions through the irreal postcapitalist city of Bliptown where time ticks sideways, artificial Bug-Eyed Monsters punish citizens for consumer-capitalist lethargy, and ultraviolence is as essential as a daily multivitamin. **208 pages $15**

BB-046 "The Million-Year Centipede" Eckhard Gerdes - Wakelin, frontman for 'The Hinge,' wrote a poem so prophetic that to ignore it dooms a person to drown in blood. **130 pages $12**

BB-047 "Sausagey Santa" Carlton Mellick III - A bizarro Christmas tale featuring Santa as a piratey mutant with a body made of sausages. 124 pages $10

BB-048 "Misadventures in a Thumbnail Universe" Vincent Sakowski - Dive deep into the surreal and satirical realms of neo-classical Blender Fiction, filled with television shoes and flesh-filled skies. **120 pages $10**

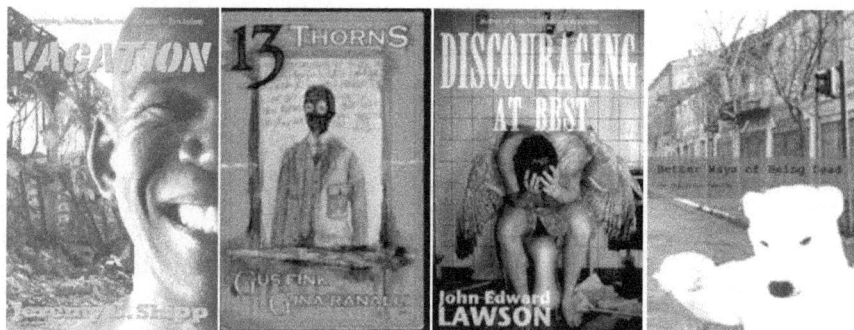

BB-049 "Vacation" Jeremy C. Shipp - Blueblood Bernard Johnson leaved his boring life behind to go on The Vacation, a year-long corporate sponsored odyssey. But instead of seeing the world, Bernard is captured by terrorists, becomes a key figure in secret drug wars, and, worse, doesn't once miss his secure American Dream. **160 pages $14**

BB-051 "13 Thorns" Gina Ranalli - Thirteen tales of twisted, bizarro horror. **240 pages $13**

BB-050 "Discouraging at Best" John Edward Lawson - A collection where the absurdity of the mundane expands exponentially creating a tidal wave that sweeps reason away. For those who enjoy satire, bizarro, or a good old-fashioned slap to the senses. **208 pages $15**

BB-052 "Better Ways of Being Dead" Christian TeBordo - In this class, the students have to keep one palm down on the table at all times, and listen to lectures about a panda who speaks Chinese. **216 pages $14**

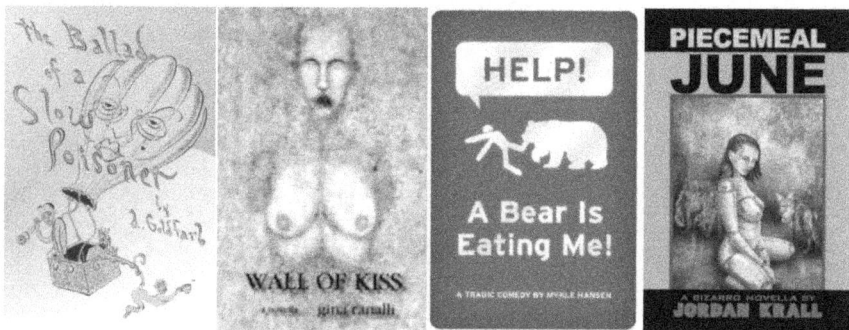

BB-053 "Ballad of a Slow Poisoner" Andrew Goldfarb Millford Mutterwurst sat down on a Tuesday to take his afternoon tea, and made the unpleasant discovery that his elbows were becoming flatter. **128 pages $10**

BB-054 "Wall of Kiss" Gina Ranalli - A woman... A wall... Sometimes love blooms in the strangest of places. **108 pages $9**

BB-055 "HELP! A Bear is Eating Me" Mykle Hansen - The bizarro, heartwarming, magical tale of poor planning, hubris and severe blood loss... **150 pages $11**

BB-056 "Piecemeal June" Jordan Krall - A man falls in love with a living sex doll, but with love comes danger when her creator comes after her with crab-squid assassins. **90 pages $9**

BB-057 "Laredo" Tony Rauch - Dreamlike, surreal stories by Tony Rauch. **180 pages $12**

BB-058 "The Overwhelming Urge" Andersen Prunty - A collection of bizarro tales by Andersen Prunty. **150 pages $11**

BB-059 "Adolf in Wonderland" Carlton Mellick III - A dreamlike adventure that takes a young descendant of Adolf Hitler's design and sends him down the rabbit hole into a world of imperfection and disorder. **180 pages $11**

BB-060 "Super Cell Anemia" Duncan B. Barlow - "Unrelentingly bizarre and mysterious, unsettling in all the right ways..." - Brian Evenson. **180 pages $12**

BB-061 "Ultra Fuckers" Carlton Mellick III - Absurdist suburban horror about a couple who enter an upper middle class gated community but can't find their way out. **108 pages $9**

BB-062 "House of Houses" Kevin L. Donihe - An odd man wants to marry his house. Unfortunately, all of the houses in the world collapse at the same time in the Great House Holocaust. Now he must travel to House Heaven to find his departed fiancee. **172 pages $11**

BB-063 "Necro Sex Machine" Andre Duza - The Dead Bitch returns in this follow-up to the bizarro zombie epic Dead Bitch Army. **400 pages $16**

BB-064 "Squid Pulp Blues" Jordan Krall - In these three bizarro-noir novellas, the reader is thrown into a world of murderers, drugs made from squid parts, deformed gun-toting veterans, and a mischievous apocalyptic donkey. **204 pages $12**

BB-065 "Jack and Mr. Grin" Andersen Prunty - "When Mr. Grin calls you can hear a smile in his voice. Not a warm and friendly smile, but the kind that seizes your spine in fear. You don't need to pay your phone bill to hear it. That smile is in every line of Prunty's prose." - Tom Bradley. **208 pages $12**

BB-066 "Cybernetrix" Carlton Mellick III - What would you do if your normal everyday world was slowly mutating into the video game world from Tron? **212 pages $12**

BB-067 "Lemur" Tom Bradley - Spencer Sproul is a would-be serial-killing bus boy who can't manage to murder, injure, or even scare anybody. However, there are other ways to do damage to far more people and do it legally... **120 pages $12**

BB-068 "Cocoon of Terror" Jason Earls - Decapitated corpses...a sculpture of terror...Zelian's masterpiece, his Cocoon of Terror, will trigger a supernatural disaster for everyone on Earth. **196 pages $14**

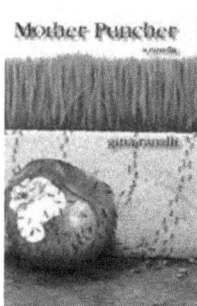

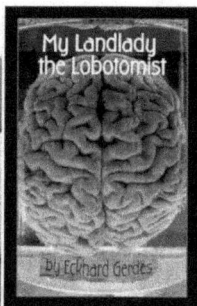

BB-069 "Mother Puncher" Gina Ranalli - The world has become tragically over-populated and now the government strongly opposes procreation. Ed is employed by the government as a mother-puncher. He doesn't relish his job, but he knows it has to be done and he knows he's the best one to do it. **120 pages $9**

BB-070 "My Landlady the Lobotomist" Eckhard Gerdes - The brains of past tenants line the shelves of my boarding house, soaking in a mysterious elixir. One more slip-up and the landlady might just add my frontal lobe to her collection. **116 pages $12**

BB-071 "CPR for Dummies" Mickey Z. - This hilarious freakshow at the world's end is the fragmented, sobering debut novel by acclaimed nonfiction author Mickey Z. **216 pages $14**

BB-072 "Zerostrata" Andersen Prunty - Hansel Nothing lives in a tree house, suffers from memory loss, has a very eccentric family, and falls in love with a woman who runs naked through the woods every night. **144 pages $11**

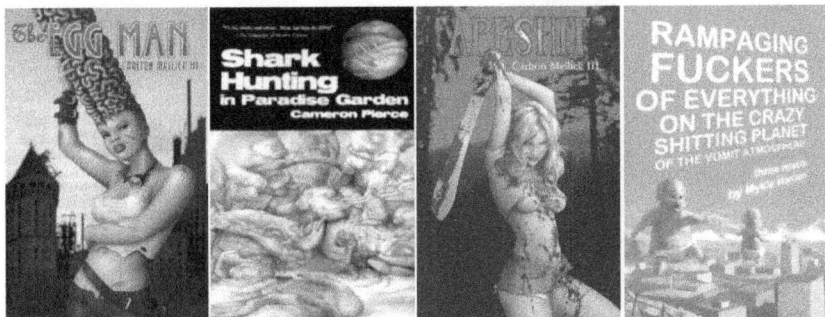

BB-073 "The Egg Man" Carlton Mellick III - It is a world where humans
reproduce like insects. Children are the property of corporations, and having an enormous ten-foot brain implanted into your skull is a grotesque sexual fetish. Mellick's industrial urban dystopia is one of his darkest and grittiest to date. **184 pages $11**

BB-074 "Shark Hunting in Paradise Garden" Cameron Pierce - A
group of strange humanoid religious fanatics travel back in time to the Garden of Eden to discover it is invested with hundreds of giant flying maneating sharks. **150 pages $10**

BB-075 "Apeshit" Carlton Mellick III - Friday the 13th meets Visitor Q. Six
hipster teens go to a cabin in the woods inhabited by a deformed killer. An incredibly fucked-up parody of B-horror movies with a bizarro slant. **192 pages $12**

BB-076 "Rampaging Fuckers of Everything on the Crazy Shitting Planet of the Vomit At smosphere" Mykle Hansen - 3 bizarro satires. Monster
Cocks, Journey to the Center of Agnes Cuddlebottom, and Crazy Shitting Planet. **228 pages $12**

BB-077 "The Kissing Bug" Daniel Scott Buck - In the tradition of Roald
Dahl, Tim Burton, and Edward Gorey, comes this bizarro anti-war children's story about a bohemian conenose kissing bug who falls in love with a human woman. **116 pages $10**

BB-078 "MachoPoni" Lotus Rose - It's My Little Pony... *Bizarro* style! A long
time ago Poniworld was split in two. On one side of the Jagged Line is the Pastel Kingdom, a magical land of music, parties, and positivity. On the other side of the Jagged Line is Dark Kingdom inhabited by an army of undead ponies. **148 pages $11**

BB-079 "The Faggiest Vampire" Carlton Mellick III - A Roald Dahl-
esque children's story about two faggy vampires who partake in a mustache competition to find out which one is truly the faggiest. **104 pages $10**

BB-080 "Sky Tongues" Gina Ranalli - The autobiography of Sky Tongues,
the biracial hermaphrodite actress with tongues for fingers. Follow her strange life story as she rises from freak to fame. **204 pages $12**

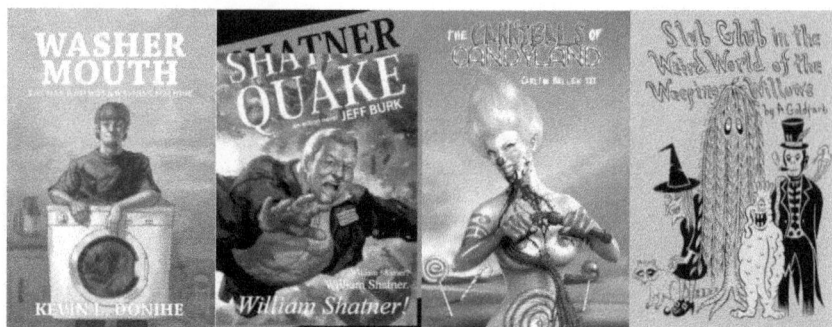

BB-081 "Washer Mouth" Kevin L. Donihe - A washing machine becomes human and pursues his dream of meeting his favorite soap opera star. **244 pages $11**

BB-082 "Shatnerquake" Jeff Burk - All of the characters ever played by William Shatner are suddenly sucked into our world. Their mission: hunt down and destroy the real William Shatner. **100 pages $10**

BB-083 "The Cannibals of Candyland" Carlton Mellick III - There exists a race of cannibals that are made of candy. They live in an underground world made out of candy. One man has dedicated his life to killing them all. **170 pages $11**

BB-084 "Slub Glub in the Weird World of the Weeping Willows" Andrew Goldfarb - The charming tale of a blue glob named Slub Glub who helps the weeping willows whose tears are flooding the earth. There are also hyenas, ghosts, and a voodoo priest **100 pages $10**

BB-085 "Super Fetus" Adam Pepper - Try to abort this fetus and he'll kick your ass! **104 pages $10**

BB-086 "Fistful of Feet" Jordan Krall - A bizarro tribute to spaghetti westerns, featuring Cthulhu-worshipping Indians, a woman with four feet, a crazed gunman who is obsessed with sucking on candy, Syphilis-ridden mutants, sexually transmitted tattoos, and a house devoted to the freakiest fetishes. **228 pages $12**

BB-087 "Ass Goblins of Auschwitz" Cameron Pierce - It's Monty Python meets Nazi exploitation in a surreal nightmare as can only be imagined by Bizarro author Cameron Pierce. **104 pages $10**

BB-088 "Silent Weapons for Quiet Wars" Cody Goodfellow - "This is high-end psychological surrealist horror meets bottom-feeding low-life crime in a techno-thrilling science fiction world full of Lovecraft and magic..." -John Skipp **212 pages $12**

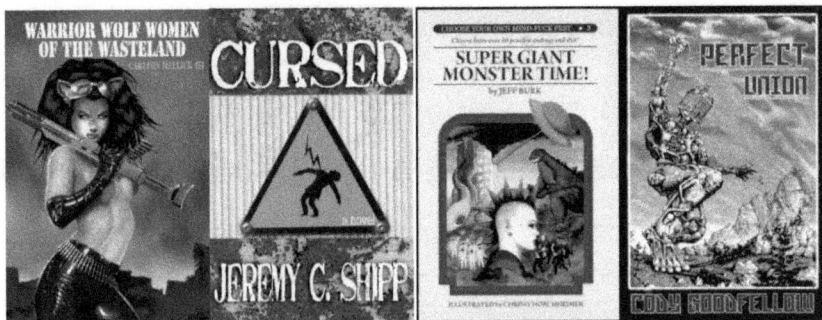

BB-089 "Warrior Wolf Women of the Wasteland" Carlton Mellick III
Road Warrior Werewolves versus McDonaldland Mutants...post-apocalyptic fiction has never been quite like this. **316 pages $13**

BB-090 "Cursed" Jeremy C Shipp - The story of a group of characters who believe they are cursed and attempt to figure out who cursed them and why. A tale of stylish absurdism and suspenseful horror. **218 pages $15**

BB-091 "Super Giant Monster Time" Jeff Burk - A tribute to choose your own adventures and Godzilla movies. Will you escape the giant monsters that are rampaging the fuck out of your city and shit? Or will you join the mob of alien-controlled punk rockers causing chaos in the streets? What happens next depends on you. **188 pages $12**

BB-092 "Perfect Union" Cody Goodfellow - "Cronenberg's THE FLY on a grand scale: human/insect gene-spliced body horror, where the human hive politics are as shocking as the gore." -John Skipp. **272 pages $13**

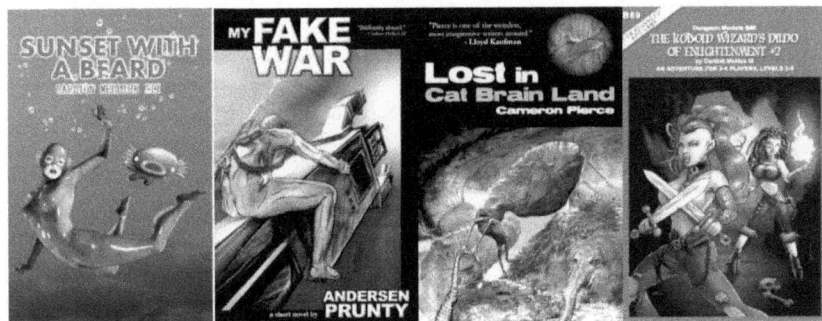

BB-093 "Sunset with a Beard" Carlton Mellick III - 14 stories of surreal science fiction. **200 pages $12**

BB-094 "My Fake War" Andersen Prunty - The absurd tale of an unlikely soldier forced to fight a war that, quite possibly, does not exist. It's Rambo meets Waiting for Godot in this subversive satire of American values and the scope of the human imagination. **128 pages $11**

BB-095 "Lost in Cat Brain Land" Cameron Pierce - Sad stories from a surreal world. A fascist mustache, the ghost of Franz Kafka, a desert inside a dead cat. Primordial entities mourn the death of their child. The desperate serve tea to mysterious creatures. A hopeless romantic falls in love with a pterodactyl. And much more. **152 pages $11**

BB-096 "The Kobold Wizard's Dildo of Enlightenment +2" Carlton Mellick III - A Dungeons and Dragons parody about a group of people who learn they are only made up characters in an AD&D campaign and must find a way to resist their nerdy teenaged players and retarded dungeon master in order to survive. 232 **pages $12**

ORDER FORM

TITLES	QTY	PRICE	TOTAL

Please make checks and moneyorders payable to ROSE O'KEEFE / BIZARRO BOOKS in U.S. funds only. Please don't send bad checks! Allow 2-6 weeks for delivery. International orders may take longer. If you'd like to pay online via PAYPAL.COM, send payments to publisher@eraserheadpress.com.

SHIPPING: US ORDERS - $2 for the first book, $1 for each additional book. For priority shipping, add an additional $4. INT'L ORDERS - $5 for the first book, $3 for each additional book. Add an additional $5 per book for global priority shipping.

Send payment to:

BIZARRO BOOKS
  C/O Rose O'Keefe
  205 NE Bryant
  Portland, OR 97211

Address

City   State   Zip

Email   Phone

www.ingramcontent.com/pod-product-compliance
Lightning Source LLC
LaVergne TN
LVHW011335080426
835513LV00006B/353